LIGHT FOR MY PATH

The New Code of Canon Law for Religious

Digest • Source Material • Commentary

LIGHT FOR MY PATH

The New Code of Canon Law for Religious

Digest • Source Material • Commentary

Austin Flannery, OP / Laurence Collins, OP

Michael Glazier, Inc.
Wilmington, Delaware

First published in 1983 by Michael Glazier, Inc., 1723 Delaware Avenue, Wilmington, Delaware 19806 and Dominican Publications, Upper Dorset Street, Dublin 1, Ireland.

Library of Congress Catalog Card Number: 83-81158
International Standard Book Numbers:
  0-89453-334-7 (Michael Glazier, Inc., Paper)
  0-89453-335-5 (Michael Glazier, Inc., Cloth)
  0-907271-22-7 (Dominican Publications)

Typography by Susan Pickett

Printed in the United States of America

For
Paul Bowe, OP
in
Friendship

CONTENTS

INTRODUCTION

This book contains:

(a) A digest of that portion of the new Code of Canon Law, *Codex Juris Canonici,* which deals with 'Institutes of Consecrated Life' and 'Societies of Apostolic Life.' The terms, 'Institutes of Consecrated Life' is of fairly recent coinage and it covers 'Religious Institutes' (religious orders and congregations) and 'Secular Institutes,' plus two categories of consecrated persons: virgins and hermits.

The portion of the Code in question is from Canon 573 through Canon 746. To this is added, in an appendix, a digest of short sections of the Code on elections and on authority. The substance of other Canons and portions of Canons, including Canons from 'book' five, on property, is given as the need arises in the digest of or commentary on Canons 573 through 746.

(b) An extensive selection of supplementary documentation of passages from the documents of the Second Council of the Vatican and from subsequent Papal and other Roman documents, all of them of the greatest relevance to the section of the Code dealt with in this book. The passages are interspersed through the book, each one following directly after the digest of the Canon on which it has a bearing.

Not only do they throw light on the Canons, they considerably enrich their meaning. Some of them have been selected because they are the direct sources of Canons, others because they provide the thinking on the theology of institutes of consecrated life and of societies of apostolic life and of the thinking on their spirituality and apostolate which informs the Canons.

The documents range from the *Dogmatic Constitution on the Church* (1964) to the documents on *The Contemplative Dimension of Religious Life* and on *Religious and Human Advancement,* (both 1981). The selection amounts to an invaluable compendium of the Church's reflection on the institutes of consecrated life and on societies of apostolic life at Vatican II and since. (A word about the terminology used in the documents: for the most part, the words 'religious' or 'religious life' as they are used in the documents refer to all of the institutes covered in the new code. The present terminology had not yet come into use. See Introduction to the Commentary.)

(c) An Introduction and a brief canonical commentary on selected Canons. The commentary would have been a good deal longer were it not for the abundance of commentary already contained in the passages from the documents.

In compiling the book we have had the needs of the

less technically expert and less technically curious reader in mind. Thus, in the digest of the Canons, we have endeavored to convey the Canons in substance rather than in intricate detail. There is less concentration on more technical matters which are of less than riveting concern for most readers, or of very infrequent concern.

One example may suffice to illustrate our approach. Canon 624, 1. states that superiors hold office for a fixed time. That is the substance of the Canon. But it goes on to say that the duration decided upon must be in keeping with the nature and the needs of the institute and that some institutes may decide not to assign a fixed term for their superior general. Our digest does not give these details.

Such details are of course important, but are not normally of concern for the non-specialist, except — usually in the context of a general or provincial chapter — when the need may arise to submit the text of the Code to closer scrutiny. Only the full text of the Code will meet the needs of the specialist or will stand the kind of close scrutiny just referred to. In fact, only the Latin text can fully meet the needs of the expert or bear up under really close scrutiny, for only the Latin text is official as Cardinal Casaroli, the Secretary of State at the Vatican, said when the new Code was promulgated on 28 January, 1983.

The section of the code reproduced here in digest form does not, of course, exhaust all that the Code has to say to members of institutes of consecrated life and of societies of apostolic life. One hopes that readers of this book will feel encouraged to read the full text of the code in Latin, or, when it becomes available, in

English. This book's commentary and documentation can also be used in conjunction with the full text of the section of the code given here in digest form. One hopes, lastly, that readers hitherto unfamiliar with all of the documents quoted will want to read them in full.

Austin Flannery, O.P.

ABBREVIATIONS OF THE TITLES OF DOCUMENTS QUOTED

Consecration to a Life of Virginity: Sacred Congregation for Divine Worship, *Introduction to the Rite of Consecration to a Life of Virginity, Mos virgines consecrandi*, 31 May, 1970. Text in *Vatican II: More Postconciliar Documents*, edited by Austin Flannery, O.P. Hereafter referred to as 'Flannery 2.'

Const. on the Church: Vatican II, *Dogmatic Constitution on the Church, Lumen Gentium*, 21 November, 1964. Text in *Vatican II: Conciliar and Postconciliar Documents*, edited by Austin Flannery, O.P. Hereafter referred to as 'Flannery 1.'

Contemplative Dimension: Sacred Congregation for Religious and Secular Institutes, *The Contemplative Dimension of Religious Life, La Plenaria* January, 1981. Text in Flannery 2.

Contemplative Life: Sacred Congregation for Religious and Secular Institutes, *Instruction on the Contemplative Life and on the Enclosure of Nuns, Venite seorsum*, 15 August, 1969. Text in Flannery 1.

Decree on Bishops: Vatican II, *Decree on the Pastoral Office of Bishops in the Church, Christus Dominus*, 28 October, 1965. Text in Flannery 1.

Decree on Religious Life: Vatican II, *Decree on the Up-to-date Renewal of Religious Life, Perfectae Caritatis*, 28 October, 1965. Text in Flannery 1.

Exhortation on Religious Life: Paul VI, *Apostolic Exhortation on the Renewal of Religious Life, Evangelica Testificatio*, 29 June, 1971. Text in Flannery 1.

Instruction on Contemplative Life: Sacred Congregation for Religious and Secular Institutes, *Instruction on Contemplative Life, Veni Seorsum*, 15 August, 1969. Text in Flannery 1.

Instruction on Renewal: Sacred Congregation for Religious and Secular Institutes, *Instruction on the Renewal of Religious Life, Renovationis Causam*, 6 January, 1969. Text in Flannery 1.

Mutual Relations: Sacred Congregation for Religious and Secular Institutes, *Directives for Mutual Relations between Bishops and Religious in the Church, Mutuae Relationes*, 23 April, 1978. Text in Flannery 2.

Norms on Religious Life: Paul VI, *Norms for Implementing the Decree on the Up-to-date Renewal* *of Religious Life* usually referred to as *Ecclesiae Sanctae II* (see below). Text in Flannery 1.

Norms on Bishops: Paul VI, *Apostolic Letter, Written Motu Proprio, on the Implementation of the Decrees Christus Presbyterorum Ordinis.* The letter, *Ecclesiae Sanctae*, gave its name to the actual norms for the implementation of the decrees. The norms for the implementation of the decrees on bishops and priests is usually referred to as *Ecclesiae Sanctae I*, 6 August, 1966. Text in Flannery 1.

Religious and Human Advancement: Sacred Congregation for Religious and Secular Institutes, *Religious and Human Advancement, Le scelte evangeliche*, January, 1981. Text in Flannery 2.

THE PREPARATION OF THE NEW CODE

Introduction

On January 25th, 1983, Pope John Paul II promulgated the new Code of Canon Law. It comes into force on the first day of Advent, November 27th, 1983. The section on 'Institutes of Consecrated Life and Societies of Apostolic Life' is the third part of the second book on the 'People of God.' The first part is on the 'Christian Faithful,' the second part treats of the 'Hierarchical Constitution of the Church,' while the third part is the section which will be considered here.

Book II   The People of God.   Cans. 204-746
  Part I   The Christian Faithful   Cans. 204-329
  Part II   The Hierarchical Constitution of the Church   Cans. 330-572
  Part III   Institutes of Consecrated Life and Societies of Apostolic Life   Cans. 573-746

The Preparation of the Text

On the feast of the Conversion of St. Paul, January 25th, 1959, Pope John XXIII convoked the ecumenical council. At the same time, he called the Synod of Rome and announced that the Code of Canon Law would be updated.

The next few years were taken up with preparation for the Council, but, in March, 1963, Pope John established the Pontifical Commission for the Revision of the Code of Canon Law. When this group met in November, 1963, during the Second Session of the Council, it was decided that the work of revision should be adjourned until the Council was over. However, on April 17th, 1964, Paul VI established a consultative commission.

One of the first major questions facing the Commission was to decide whether there should be one code for the Universal Church, or whether separate codes should be prepared for the Latin and Oriental churches. It was decided to draft separate codes for the East and West.

In 1966, the Commission drew up a number of principles to guide the work of the revision. These ten principles were subsequently approved by the Synod of Bishops in 1967. A number of sub-commissions were established and eventually the plan of the new Code was drawn up. It differs considerably from the 1917 Code. There are seven books: (1) General Norms, (2) The People of God, (3) The Church's Teaching Mission, (4) The Sanctifying Mission of the Church, (5) The Temporal Goods of the Church, (6) Penal Law, (7) Procedure.

One of the sub-commissions was assigned the task of drafting the law for "religious." The title for the sub-commission was taken from chapter six of the Constitution on the Church "Lumen Gentium." In this chapter on religious the Council included all those who profess publicly in the Church, by vows or other sacred promises, the evangelical counsels of chastity, poverty and obedience. The council had given a theological description of religious. Secular institutes were very unhappy about this. As a result, the Council's *Decree on the Up-to-date Renewal of Religious Life, Perfectae Caritatis* (hereafter referred to as the *Decree on Religious Life*) clearly stated that secular institutes were not religious. After the fourth meeting of the study-group in April, 1968, the term 'religious' in its title was changed to 'Institutes of Perfection,' so as to include secular institutes and others whose members did not wish to be considered religious. But neither was this title considered satisfactory and it was consequently changed to the present title, 'Institutes of Consecrated Life.'

In addition to the general principles laid down by the Synod in 1967 (*Communicationes I*, 1969 pp. 77-85), a number of additional guidelines were drawn up to guide the drafting of the new canons on institutes of consecrated life. These principles were:

(1) The gift of consecrated life was to be aptly expressed. Juridical norms, though they do not exhaust the richness of the consecrated life, must foster the growth of this vocation.

(2) The canons should encourage each institute to preserve the Founder's spirit and help the members to keep alive their spiritual heritage.

(3) While the essential elements of consecrated life are to be clearly set down, the new law was to be flexible in its adaptation to the conditions of the life and work of the institutes.

(4) There must be greater participation by the members in the life and government of the institute. Methods of representation and participation in government must be developed in each institute. Authority is not to be concentrated for too long a period in the hands of any one individual.

Other principles were set out in the report of the study group which guided the work of the revision. (Beyer, Jean, "Institutes of Perfection in the New Law of the Church" in *The Way, Supplement,* 13[1971]).

(1) General norms should be concerned only with matters which are appropriate to all: the diversity of institutes should be recognised.

(2) The greatest possible harmony should exist between the common law and the particular law of each institute so that the common law should lay down what is strictly necessary.

(3) Provision should be made in the general law for the application of the principle of subsidiarity.

(4) The dignity, rights and responsibilities of the human person should be properly recognised.

(5) There should be no discrimination between institutes of men and women. However, it is unfortunate that this principle of equality was not acknowledged in practice. There were no female religious representatives on the subcommission which drafted this section of the new law.

On February 2nd, 1977, the subcommission on Institutes of Consecrated Life finished its draft of the canons. It was sent to the various groups for comments and suggestions.

In this draft general preliminary canons were placed at the beginning of the schema. They were followed by the first part which contained 82 canons applicable to every type of consecrated life, religious institutes, societies of common life and secular institutes. The second part contained 38 canons in which institutes were distinguished typologically with specific legislation for each type.

The subcommission had certainly attempted to express in legislation the teaching of the Council. Many of the phrases used in the canons were taken from the *Dogmatic Constitution on the Church, Lumen Gentium*, (hereafter referred to as *Const. on the Church*) and the *Decree on Religious Life*. The Council documents had been criticised for their treatment of the religious life. Part one of the draft was in turn criticised for reducing religious institutes to a common denominator, making insufficient distinction between them and secular institutes. The Council documents had dealt with religious primarily from a theological viewpoint, while the law is primarily concerned with expressing legal and juridical terms. At the same time, however, it was accepted that legislation must be based on sound doctrine. Major criticisms of the 1977 draft were levelled at the typological classification of institutes in part two, a classification based on the *Const. on the Church*, no. 46 and at the uniformity of the general legislation and its tendency to reduce all to the same level. The typological classification of institutes of consecrated life is found in the *Decree on Religious Life*, nos. 7 to 11 and is as follows: contemplative religious (7), religious devoted to various forms of the apostolate (8), monastic life (9), secular institutes (11). Because of the uniformity of the legislation, such terms as 'profession,' 'novice,' 'superior' were not used. In their place, the terms 'coaptation,' 'newly-received' and 'moderator' were introduced. The dropping of the traditional terminology was criticised by theologians and canonists.

There were strong negative criticisms especially from the religious superiors consulted and that draft was rejected.

A new subcommission was formed with the task of revising the 1977 draft in the light of the comments received. By the summer of 1980 the text had been redrafted and sent to the Cardinals who were members of the Pontifical Commission for the Revision of the Code. Their observations were discussed in a plenary session of the commission and the final text was sent to the Pope. The new subcommission, while recognising the importance of doctrine in drafting the law particularly in the earlier canons, has been consistently more juridical. Terms like superior, novice and profession are found in the text and the levelling process feared by some critics of the 1977 draft is avoided. In the new Code, Can. 577 draws on the words of the *Const. on the Church*, no. 46, but the text is no longer used as a typological basis for the classification of institutes. It acknowledges that the different formal goals of institutes of Consecrated Life are different ways of imitating Christ.

There are now two sections: Section I is on Institutes of Consecrated Life, Section II is on Societies of Apostolic Life.

Section I is divided into Title I on Norms common to all Institutes of Consecrated Life. Title II contains the specific legislation for religious institutes properly so called. Title III is concerned with secular institutes.

Laurence Collins, O.P

INSTITUTES OF CONSECRATED LIFE AND SOCIETIES OF APOSTOLIC LIFE

SECTION I: INSTITUTES OF CONSECRATED LIFE

Title I: Norms Common to All Institutes of Consecrated Life

Commentary

The title 'Institutes of Consecrated Life' covers religious institutes and secular institutes. Societies of Apostolic Life are treated in section II. Even though many such societies profess the three evangelical counsels, they are treated separately from the institutes of religious life because their members do not take public vows and from secular institutes because they live a common life.

The word 'title' is used above and throughout the Code in one of its meanings, which is 'a section of a law book.' The word 'Canon,' abbreviated throughout to 'Can.,' is also used in one of its meanings, which is 'a law, or rule, especially in ecclesiastical matters.'

Can. 573, 1. A life consecrated by profession of the evangelical counsels is stable, a way of following Christ more closely, guided by the Holy Spirit, in total dedication to and love of God and in his honour, a new and special commitment to building up the Church and to the salvation of the world, a symbol of heavenly glory.

Supplementary Documentation

Const. on the Church: They have a stable and more solidly based way of Christian life. (43) They 'consecrate themselves wholly to God, their supreme love. In a new and special way they make themselves over to God, to serve and honour him.' They 'should be dedicated also to the welfare of the entire Church. To the extent of their capabilities in keeping with the particular kind of religious life to which they are individually called . . . they have the duty of working for the implanting and strengthening of the kingdom of God and of spreading it, to the glory of the heavenly kingdom.' (44)

Introduction to the Rite of Religious Profession: Many Christians consecrate themselves to God's service and to the welfare of humankind by the sacred ties of religious life, in response to God's call. They aspire to follow Christ more closely by professing the evangelical counsels, so that the grace of baptism may be more effective in them.

Canonical Commentary

This canon synthesises the conciliar teaching and draws particularly from the *Const. on the Church,* numbers 43 and 44. The evangelical counsels form the permanent basis of the consecrated life. They have been given vastly differing juridical expression in institutions through the course of history. Structures have evolved and have been adapted to the mentality and circumstances of time, but the profession of the evangelical counsels is the characteristic feature that remains. This state is constituted by undertaking the obligation to live the evangelical counsels of chastity, poverty and obedience in an institute officially recognised by the authority of the Church.

There is close connection between baptism and the profession of the evangelical counsels. The profession of the evangelical counsels is a completion of the consecration initially made in baptism. While all the faithful are consecrated to God in baptism, those who undertake this way of life dedicate themselves publicly to God's service by a new and special title. But their profession is not just a simple renewal of baptismal promises. It is a further development and perfection of the initial baptismal commitment. It is public in so far as it is made before a legitimate representative of the ecclesial community, even if it is not accepted by the superior officially in the name of the Church, as are public vows.

The ecclesial and eschatological dimension of this way of life is also mentioned. The Church has need of the public and social testimony of the consecrated life which demonstrates that the kingdom of Christ is not of this world. It is the Church which recognises the profession from which arises the moral and juridical obligations of this state. Thus the consecrated person is completely dedicated to the service of the Church and is inserted in a special way in the mystery of the Church.

Can. 573, 2. This life-style, freely chosen, involves commitment by vows or other sacred ties to the practice of the evangelical counsels in canonically-established institutes and in conformity with their laws. It unites people to the mystery of the Church in a special way through charity.

Supplementary Documentation

Const. on the Church: Christians who pledge themselves to this kind of life bind themselves to the practice of the three evangelical counsels by vows or by other sacred ties of a similar nature. Being means and instruments of love, the evangelical counsels unite those who practice them to the Church and her mystery in a special way. (44)

Canonical Commentary

It pertains to the authority of the Church to interpret the evangelical counsels, to regulate their practice and establish stable forms of living according to them. Through the guidance of the Spirit, the Church has approved and directed the various expressions of the evangelical life which can differ widely in their structures. To guarantee an authentic interpretation of the Gospel principles, the approval of the Church is necessary. Obviously the interpretation of the counsels does not pertain exclusively to the ecclesiastical authority. Through the influence of the Spirit, the founders of different institutes have interpreted the Gospel message. But it is the authority of the Church which confers official approval on any particular interpretation. The power to regulate the practice of the evangelical counsels and establish stable forms of living these counsels flows from the authority to interpret authentically the teaching of the Gospel.

Profession must be made by a formal act by which a person becomes morally and juridically bound to the effective practice of the counsels in an institute approved by the Church.

Can. 574, 1. Consecrated life belongs to the life and holiness of the Church and therefore deserves to be approved and promoted by all.

2. Those called to it by God are granted a special grace to equip them for the Church's saving mission.

Supplementary Documentation

Const. on the Church: The state of life, then, which is constituted by the profession of the evangelical counsels, while not entering into the hierarchical structure of the Church, belongs undeniably to her life and holiness. (44)

...this sacred council gives its support and praise to men and women, brothers and sisters, who in monasteries or in schools or in missions adorn the bride of Christ.... (46)

...it should be seen as a form of life to which some Christians, both clerical and lay, are called by God so that they may contribute, each in his/her own way to the saving mission of the Church. (43)

Decree on Religious Life: The more fervently... they join themselves to Christ by the gift of their whole life, the fuller does the Church's life become and the more vigorous and fruitful its apostolate. (1)

Exhortation on Religious Life: We commend you to our dear brothers in the episcopate who, together with their collaborators in the priesthood, realize their own responsibility in regard to religious life. And we ask all the laity...to understand what a strong help you are for them in the striving for that holiness, to which they are called by their baptism in Christ, to the glory of the Father. (4)

Canonical Commentary

The profession of the evangelical counsels is recognised as a state of life in the Church. It pertains to its life and holiness and not to the hierarchical structure. Clergy are distinguished from laity because they have received the sacrament of orders. While all the faithful are consecrated to God in baptism, some have made a special consecration of their lives by the profession of the evangelical counsels in an institute approved by the Church. In this sense consecrated persons are distinguished from non-consecrated persons and both clerics and laity may be called to the state of consecrated life.

Can. 575. The evangelical counsels, based on Christ's teaching and example, are a divine gift in the Church's safe-keeping.

Supplementary Documentation

Const. on the Church: The teaching and example of Christ provide the foundation for the evangelical counsels...They constitute a gift of God which the Church has received from her Lord and which by his grace she constantly safeguards. (43)

Canonical Commentary

The Church has been given the mission to preserve and foster the counsels. Since all the faithful are bound to pursue the perfection of sanctity of their own state, they should develop the spirit of the evangelical counsels, the faithful practice of which is a witness to the holiness of the Church.

Can. 576. The Church must interpret and regulate the practice of the counsels, approving institutes and monitoring their development.

Supplementary Documentation

Const. on the Church: Guided by the Holy Spirit, Church authority has been at pains to interpret the counsels, to regulate their practice, and also to set up stable forms of living embodying them. (43)
...it is for the hierarchy to make wise laws for the regulation of the practice of the counsels.... It uses its supervisory and protective authority too to ensure that religious institutes established all over the world...may develop and flourish in accordance with the spirit of their founders. (45)

Canonical Commentary

It is for the Church to interpret the evangelical counsels, to regulate their practice and establish stable forms of living according to them. Through the guidance of the Spirit, the Church has approved and directed various forms of the evangelical life, from the heremitical and monastic life to secular institutes. The spirit of the founders and the sound traditions of the institute should be fostered.

Can. 577. There are many different institutes, differing ways of following Christ at prayer, preaching the kingdom, doing good to people or dealing with them in the world.

Supplementary Documentation

Const. on the Church: Let religious see well to it that the Church show forth Christ through them.... Christ in contemplation on the mountain, or proclaiming the kingdom of God to the multitudes, or healing the sick and maimed and converting sinners to a good life...always in obedience to the Father who sent him. (46)

Decree on Religious Life:....all those who are called by God to the practice of the evangelical counsels and who make faithful profession of them, bind themselves to the Lord in a special way. They follow Christ who, virginal and poor (Matt 8:12; Luke 9:58), redeemed and sanctified men by obedience unto death on the cross (cf. Phil 2:8). Under the impulse of love, which the Holy Spirit pours into their hearts (cf. Rom 5:5), they live more and more for Christ and for his Body, the Church (cf. Col 1:24) (1)

From the very beginning of the Church there were men and women who set out to follow Christ with greater liberty, and to imitate him more closely, by practising the evangelical counsels. They led lives dedicated to God, each in his/her own way. Many of them, under the inspiration of the Holy Spirit, became hermits or founded religious families. These the Church, by virtue of her authority, gladly accepted and approved. Thus, in keeping with the divine purpose, a wonderful variety of religious communities came into existence. (ibid.)

Canonical Commentary

It is because there are different gifts of the Spirit that there are different institutes. This is the basis for the classification of institutes outlined in the *Const. on the Church*, no. 46 and repeated in this Canon. The phrase 'or dealing with them in the world: *sive cum eis in saeculo conversantem*' was clearly added for the sake of secular institutes.

Can. 578. An institute's patrimony comprises what its founder intended to be its nature, purpose, spirit and character, with its sound traditions. These must be observed.

Supplementary Documentation

Decree on Religious Life: It is for the good of the Church that institutes have their own proper characters and functions. Therefore the spirit and aim of each founder should be faithfully accepted and retained, as indeed should each institute's sound traditions, for all of these constitute the patrimony of an institute. (2a)

Can. 579. A diocesan bishop may by formal decree establish institutes of consecrated life, having consulted the Holy See.

Supplementary Documentation

Const. on the Church: It is the task of the Church's hierarchy to nourish the people of God and to lead them to good pasture (Ezek 34:14). Accordingly it is for the hierarchy to make wise laws for the regulation of the practice of the counsels. . . . Again, in docile response to the promptings of the Holy Spirit the hierarchy accepts rules of religious life which are presented for its approval by outstanding men and women, improves them further and then officially authorises them. (45)

Can. 580. Aggregation must not involve loss of autonomy.

Canonical Commentary

Aggregation is a form of association by which one institute 'aggregates' another institute to itself, making it a 'moral member' of itself. The association is purely spiritual and by its means the 'aggregated' institute shares in the spiritual favours and liturgical privileges of the 'aggregating' institute, but does not share in juridical privileges, such as exemption. The 'aggregated' institute does not in any way become subject to the authority or jurisdiction of the other institute. There has to be a similarity in spirit and manner of life between the two institutes.

Can. 581. On dividing institutes into parts and modifying existing parts.

Canonical Commentary

The 'parts' of an institute have usually been referred to as 'provinces.' A province is a distinct 'juridical' or 'moral person' composed of at least three canonically established houses. It is governed by a 'moderator,' who is distinct from the local moderator and from the general moderator and who possesses ordinary authority — authority, that is, which is granted by law and not by delegation. The term 'region' has been applied to parts of an institute which are not distinct 'juridical persons' and consequently are not provinces. The authority of the regional moderator is delegated and consequently a regional superior is not a major superior.

Can. 582. Fusions, unions, federations, confederations are reserved to the Holy See.

Supplementary Documentation

Decree on Religious Life: Institutes and independent monasteries should, as opportunity offers and with the approval of the Holy See, form federations, if they belong in some measure to the same religious family. Failing this they should form unions, if they have almost identical constitutions and customs, have the same spirit, and especially if they are few in number. Or they should form associations if they have the same or similar active apostolates. (22)

Norms on Religious Life: The project for a union between institutes — whatever its nature may be —supposes an adequate preparation, spiritual, psychological, juridical, according to the mind of the

Decree (quoted above). For this it is often desirable that the institutes should have the help of some assistant approved by the competent authority. (39)

In such cases and circumstances, the good of the Church must be kept in view, as also the particular character of each institute and the freedom of choice left to each individual religious. (40)

Canonical Commentary

The reason for reserving all unions and federations of consecrated life to the Holy See is to prevent institutes from uniting together solely because of shortage of numbers, at a time of decreasing vocations. It is also important that the institutes be not dissimilar in spirit. 'Federation' normally refers to the grouping of monasteries. The confederation even of autonomous monasteries is reserved to the Holy See.

Can. 583. The Holy See's approval is needed for changing what has already been approved by it.

Canonical Commentary

Examples of matters which can be changed only with the Holy See's approval are the title, purpose and work of an institute.

Can. 584. Suppression of an institute and disposal of its property are reserved to the Holy See.

Supplementary Documentation

Decree on Religious Life: Institutes and monasteries which the Holy See, having consulted the local ordinaries concerned, judges not to offer any reasonable hope of further development, are to be forbidden to receive any more novices. If possible, they are to be amalgamated with more flourishing institutes or monasteries whose aims and spirit differ little from their own. (21)

Norms on Religious Life: In attempting to reach a decision concerning the suppression of an institute or monastery, the following are the criteria which, taken together, one should retain after one has taken all the circumstances into consideration: the number of members remains small, even though the institute or monastery has been in existence for many years, candidates have not been forthcoming for a long time past and most members are advanced in years....Each religious must be individually consulted beforehand, and all must be done with charity. (41)

Can. 585. An institute may itself suppress parts of itself.

Canonical Commentary

There is no need for recourse to the Holy See when there is question of suppressing existing provinces of an institute, uniting them or changing their boundaries.

Can. 586, 1. An institute's autonomy in life-style and government is acknowledged.

Supplementary Documentation

Decree on Bishops: Religious who are engaged in the external apostolate should be inspired by the spirit of their own institute, should remain faithful to the observance of their rule, and should be obedient to their superiors. (35,2)

All religious. . . are subject to the authority of the local ordinary in the following matters: public worship, without prejudice however to the diversity of rites; the care of souls; preaching to the people; the religious and moral education, catechetical instruction and liturgical formation of the faithful, especially of children. They are also subject to diocesan rules regarding the comportment proper to the clerical state and the various activities relating to the exercise of their sacred apostolate. Catholic schools conducted by religious are also subject to the local ordinaries as regards their general policy and supervision, without prejudice, however, to the right of the religious to manage them. Likewise, religious are obliged to observe all those prescriptions which episcopal councils or conferences legitimately decree as binding on all. (35,4)

Mutual Relations: There is then *an internal organization* in religious institutes which has its proper field of competency and a measure of real *autonomy*, even though in the Church this autonomy can never become *independence*. The right degree of this autonomy and its concrete delimitation of competency are contained in the common law and in the rules or constitutions of each institute. (13,c)

Canonical Commentary

The autonomy of each institute, particularly in government, is acknowledged. This refers particularly to the internal autonomy of institutes in managing their affairs. They have a right to their own discipline and to preserve their own liturgical, doctrinal and spiritual heritage. There is also an external autonomy by which the religious have the right to engage in works which are in keeping with the proper character of the institute. This autonomy is not to be identified with exemption. All religious are subject to the bishop in matters of public worship, preaching, education, catechetical instruction and clerical life, without prejudice to the external autonomy referred to above.

Can. 586, 2. A bishop should observe and safeguard an institute's autonomy.

Canonical Commentary

It is important that bishops and diocesan clergy understand the place of religious in the Church. The work which religious are invited to undertake in a diocese or in a parish should be in keeping with the charism and character of their institute.

Can. 587, 1. An institute's basic code or constitutions should contain, over and above what is listed in Canon 578, its fundamental norms of government, of the incorporation and the formation of its members and concerning the object of its sacred bonds.

2. Approval and permission to change this code come from the competent Church authority.

3. The code should combine the spiritual and the juridical, but should not be over-detailed.

4. The remaining norms should be collected in directories which the institute itself can change as occasion demands.

Supplementary Documentation

Norms on Religious Life: The general laws of every institute (constitutions, typica, rules or whatever other name is given to them) must, generally speaking, contain the following elements:

(a) The evangelical and theological principles concerning religious life and its incorporation in the Church and an apt and accurate formulation in which "the spirit and aims of the founder should be clearly recognised and faithfully preserved, as indeed should each institute's traditions, for all of these constitute the patrimony of an institute."

(b) The juridical norms necessary to define the character, aims and means employed by the institute. Such rules must not be multiplied unduly, but should always be clearly formulated. (12)

A combination of both elements, the spiritual and the juridical, is necessary, so as to ensure that the principal codes of each institute will have a solid foundation and be permeated by a spirit which is authentic and a law which is alive. Care must be taken not to produce a text which is either purely juridical or merely hortatory. (13)

From the basic text of the rules one shall exclude anything which is now out of date, or anything which may change as conditions change, or which is of purely local application. These norms which are linked with present-day life or with the physical conditions or situations of the subjects, should be entered in separate books, such as directories, books of customs or similar documents, whatever be their name. (14)

Canonical Commentary

Canon 578 had stated that an institute's patrimony comprised its sound traditions and its founder's mind and intention concerning its nature, purpose, spirit and character. The present canon states that this should form part of an institute's fundamental code or constitutions, together with its fundamental norms on government, incorporation and formation of its members and the 'proper object' of its 'sacred bonds.' By 'incorporation' is meant the process of admission to the institute and by 'proper object' is meant that to which members bind themselves when they take vows, or commit themselves by some other 'sacred bond.' (For example: 'By the vow of poverty, members renounce the right etc.')

The code or constitutions are approved by the Holy See, contain the more essential, substantive and important elements of an institute's law and may be changed only with the consent of the Holy See.

The union of the spiritual and juridical elements is needed to provide a firm foundation for the institute. However, laws are not to be multiplied unnecessarily.

Other less important norms or directives should be placed in directories, which may be more easily modified and adapted to meet changing demands of time and place.

Can. 588, 1, 2 & 3. Whether an institute is clerical or lay depends on its founder's intentions, its nature, its tradition, how the Church sees it, its membership and government.

Supplementary Documentation

Const. on the Church: This form of life has its own place in relation to the divine and hierarchical structure of the Church. Not, however, as though it were a kind of middle way between the clerical and lay conditions of life. Rather, it should be seen as a form of life to which some Christians, both clerical and lay, are called by God so that they may enjoy a special gift of grace in the life of the Church and may contribute, each in his/her own way to the saving mission of the Church. (43)

Decree on Religious Life: Lay religious life, for men and women, is a state for the profession of the evangelical counsels which is complete in itself. The holy synod holds it in high esteem, for it is so useful to the Church in the exercise of its pastoral duty of educating the young, caring for the sick, and in its other ministries. . . . The holy synod declares that there is nothing to prevent some members of institutes of brothers being admitted to holy orders — the lay character of the institute remaining intact — by provision of their general chapter and in order to meet the need for priestly administration in their houses. (10)

Canonical Commentary

1. The consecrated life is neither clerical nor lay. On the contrary, persons who are either clerical or lay can be called to this charismatic way of life. The distinction between consecrated and non-consecrated persons is

based on the profession of the evangelical counsels in an institute approved by ecclesiastical authority.

2. A clerical institute is one which undertakes the exercise of the sacred ministry. The purpose of the founder, legitimate tradition and government by clerics are also mentioned as criteria for determining a clerical order but the basis of the distinction is the exercise of the priestly ministry and the approval of the Church.

3. A lay institute is one which is recognised as such by the Church and which by its nature, character and purpose has its own work defined by the founder and legitimate tradition, without including the exercise of the priestly ministry.

Can. 589. An institute is of pontifical law if established or approved by the Holy See, of diocesan law if established by a bishop.

Can. 590, 1. Institutes are subject to the Church's supreme authority.

2. Members must obey the pope as their highest superior.

Supplementary Documentation

Const. on the Church: . . .the Roman Pontiff, by reason of his office as Vicar of Christ, namely, and as pastor of the entire Church, has full, supreme and universal power over the entire Church, a power which he can always exercise unhindered. (22)

Canonical Commentary

Institutes of consecrated life are dedicated to the service of God and of the whole Church. The Roman Pontiff has ordinary and immediate power in the universal Church. The ordinary government of the Holy See over institutes of consecrated life is exercised by the Sacred Congregation for Religious and Secular Institutes through instructions, decrees, private replies and through the approval and revision of constitutions.

2. The pope is considered to be an internal moderator. He may command in virtue of the vow of obedience, but this is a power which he rarely, if ever, uses.

Can. 591. The pope may exempt institutes from the control of local ordinaries.

Supplementary Documentation

Const. on the Church: With a view to providing better for the needs of the whole of the Lord's flock and for the sake of the general good, the pope, as primate over the entire Church, can exempt any institute of Christian perfection and its individual members from the jurisdiction of local ordinaries and subject them to himself alone. Similarly, they can be left or entrusted to the care of the appropriate patriarchal authority. Members of these institutes, however, in fulfilling the duty towards the Church inherent in their particular form of life must show respect and obedience towards bishops in accordance with canon law, both because these exercise pastoral authority in their individual churches and because this is necessary for unity and harmony in the carrying out of apostolic work. (45)

Decree on Bishops: The privilege of exemption whereby religious are reserved to the control of the supreme pontiff, or of some other ecclesiastical authority, and are exempted from the jurisdiction of bishops, relates primarily to the internal organization of their institutes. Its purpose is to ensure that everything is suitably and harmoniously arranged within them and the perfection of the religious life promoted. The privilege ensures also that the supreme pontiff may employ these religious for the good of the universal Church, or that some other competent authority may do so for the good of the churches under its jurisdiction. This exemption, however, does not prevent religious being subject to the jurisdiction of the bishops. . . in accordance with the general law, insofar as is required for the performance of their pastoral duties and the proper care of souls. (35,3)

Mutual Relations: Therefore exempt religious institutes. . .should cultivate docility to the Roman Pontiff and to the bishops, placing their liberty and apostolic zeal at their disposal with good will and in conformity with religious obedience. Similarly, they should with full awareness and zeal apply themselves to the task of creating and manifesting in the diocesan family the specific witness and genuine mission of their institute. (22)

Canonical Commentary

The *Const. on the Church*, no. 35 (see above) reaffirmed the principle of exemption. The *Decree on Bishops* states (no. 35,3, see above) that exemption applies primarily to the internal autonomy of these institutes. It is the internal autonomy of religious institutes which is emphasised today. But the identity of each institute flows from its special charism and superiors must maintain this identity in their apostolic choices. The internal autonomy of institutes, even of diocesan law, is to be recognised (Can. 586, 1). This autonomy is necessary in order to safeguard the charism of the institute. While the consecrated life is inserted in the ecclesial and pastoral mission of the Church, it must maintain its own proper identity and mission. Thus *external* autonomy for the fulfillment of specialised apostolates and ministries is recognised. However, the apostolate of all religious, even those who are exempt, must be inserted into the life of the Church. The bishop is pastor of the local church and all religious are subject to him in public worship, preaching, education, catechetical instruction and clerical life.

Can. 592, 1. Superiors general should report to the Holy See on their institutes.

2. They should ensure members' observance of pertinent documents of the Holy See.

Supplementary Documentation

Const. on the Church: Guided by the Holy Spirit, Church authority has been at pains to give a right interpretation of the counsels, to regulate their practice, and also to set up stable forms of living embodying them. (43)

Can. 593. Institutes of pontifical law are subject to the Holy See for internal discipline.

Canonical Commentary

It is in their internal government and discipline that institutes of pontifical law are subject to the Holy See immediately and exclusively, with due regard for the directives in Can. 586. Such institutes are subject to bishops in matters which have to do with the care of souls, the exercise of public worship and other works of the apostolate. See Can. 678, 1, 2 and 3. See also documents quoted under Cans. 591 and 594.

Can. 594. An institute of diocesan law is subject to the diocesan bishop, with due regard for Can. 586.

Supplementary Documentation

Const. on the Church: . . . the bishops received the charge of the community, presiding in God's stead over the flock of which they are the shepherds in that they are teachers of doctrine, ministers of sacred worship and holders of office in government. (20)

Decree on Bishops: Religious should at all times treat the bishops, as successors of the apostles, with loyal respect and reverence. (35)

Canonical Commentary

The bishop is to take care of institutes of diocesan law, but must respect the character and rightful autonomy of each institute.

Can. 595, 1, 2. The diocesan bishop of the principal foundation approves constitutions, confirms changes made in them (unless the Holy See has been involved), handles major transactions and sometimes dispenses from constitutions.

Canonical Commentary

Diocesan bishops are considered to be external superiors of institutes of diocesan law, but not internal superiors. The bishop of the principal foundation need not necessarily be the bishop of the place of origin of the institute. If the institute has spread to other dioceses, their bishops need to be consulted, which does not mean that their consent is necessarily required. A diocesan bishop may grant dispensations from constitutions in individual cases.

Can. 596, 1. The power of superiors and chapters is as defined in the general law and the constitutions.

2. They also have the ecclesiastical power of government for the internal and the external forum in clerical institutes of pontifical law.

3. Canons 131, 133, 137-144 apply to no. 1. See Appendix.

Supplementary Documentation

Mutual Relations: Superiors fulfil their duty of service and leadership within the religious Institute in conformity with its distinctive character. Their authority proceeds from the Spirit of the Lord in connection with the sacred Hierarchy, which has granted canonical erection to the Institute and authentically affirmed its specific mission.

Now, from the fact that the *prophetic, priestly* and *royal* condition is common to all the People of God (LG 9, 10, 34, 35, 36), it seems useful to outline the competency of religious authority, by comparing it, analogically, with the threefold function of the pastoral ministry, namely that of teaching, sanctifying and governing, without however confusing one authority with the other, or equating them:

(a) As regards *the duty of teaching*: Religious Superiors have the competency or authority of *spiritual directors* according to the evangelical tradition of their Institute. Therefore, in this context they must impart to the Congregation as a whole or to each one of its communities, a real *'spiritual direction,'* in agreement with the authentic teaching of the Hierarchy, and fully aware of the fact that they are performing a duty of grave responsibility within the form of life laid down by the Founder.

(b) As to *the office of sanctifying*: Superiors have a special competency, as well as the responsibility, of *'perfecting,'* in various ways, the life of charity, within the rule of the Institute, either in what refers to the initial and ongoing formation of their brethren, or to the communal and personal fidelity in the practice of the Evangelical Counsels according to the Rule. This duty, conscientiously performed, is considered by the Supreme Pontiff and the Bishops as a valuable help in the fulfilment of their fundamental ministry of sanctification.

(c) As to *the office of governing*: Superiors must organise the life of the community, distribute offices to its members, take care of the special mission of the Institute, develop it and work at its effective insertion into the ecclesial activity, under the direction of the Bishop.

There is, then, *an internal organisation* in relig-ious Institutes which has its proper field of compet-ency and a measure of real *autonomy*, even though in the Church this autonomy can never become *independence*. The right degree of this autonomy and its concrete delimitation of competency are con-tained in the common law and in the Rules or Con-stitutions of each Institute.

Can. 597, 1, 2. For admission to an institute a person must be a Catholic, with the right intention, requisite qualities and preparation and with no 'impediment.'

Can. 598, 1, 2. An institute must define in its constitu-tions how its members are to observe the counsels and they for their part must comply.

Can. 599. Chastity, involving perfect continence, is a sign of heaven and a source of rich spiritual fruit.

Supplementary Documentation

Decree on Religious Life: Chastity "for the sake of the kingdom of heaven" (Matt 19:22), which relig-ious profess, must be esteemed an exceptional gift of grace. It uniquely frees the human heart (1 Cor 7:32-35), so that it becomes more fervent in love for God and for humankind. For this reason it is a special symbol of heavenly benefits, and for relig-ious it is a most effective means of dedicating themselves wholeheartedly to the divine service and the works of the apostolate. (12)

Can. 600. Poverty implies a life poor in spirit and in reality, industrious and sober in style, dependent and limited in the use of property.

Supplementary Documentation

Decree on Religious Life: Voluntary poverty, in the footsteps of Christ, is a symbol of Christ which is much esteemed nowadays. . . . It enables [people] to share in the poverty of Christ who for our sake became poor, though he was rich, so that we might become rich through his poverty.

With regard to religious poverty, it is by no means enough to be subject to superiors in the use of poverty. Religious should be poor in fact and in spirit, having their treasures in heaven.

They should, in their own assigned tasks, consider themselves bound by the common law of labour. . . . (13)

Can. 601. Obedience in faith and love in imitation of Christ obliges to submission of will to superiors, who take God's place when giving directives in accordance with the constitutions.

Supplementary Documentation

Decree on Religious Life: By their profession of obedience, religious offer the full dedication of their own wills as a sacrifice of themselves to God, and by this means they are united more permanently and securely with God's saving will. After the example of Jesus Christ, who came to do his Father's will and "taking the form of a servant" (Phil 2:7) learned obedience through what he suffered, religious moved by the Holy Spirit subject themselves in faith to those who hold God's place, their superiors.... Religious therefore should be humbly submissive to their superiors, in a spirit of faith and love for God's will, and in accordance with their rules and constitutions. (14)

Can. 602. The organization of the family-like life of the members of an institute should help them fulfil their vocation and should be an example of universal reconciliation in Christ.

Supplementary Documentation

Exhortation on Religious Life: Even if — like every Christian — you are imperfect, you nevertheless intend to create surroundings which are favorable to the spiritual progress of each member of the community. How can this happen unless you deepen in the Lord your relationships, even the most ordinary ones, with your sisters/brothers? Let us not forget that charity must be as it were an active hope for what others can become with the help of our support. The mark of its genuineness is joyful simplicity whereby all strive to understand what each one has at heart. If certain religious give the impression of having allowed themselves to be crushed by their community life, which ought instead to have made them expand and develop, does this perhaps happen because this community life lacks that understanding cordiality which nourishes hope? There is no doubt that community spirit, relationships of friendship and brotherly/sisterly cooperation in the same apostolate, as well as mutual support in a shared life for a better service of Christ, are so many valuable factors in this daily progress. (39)

Can. 603, 1. The Church recognises the heremetical way of life, devoted to the praise of God and the salvation of souls, in prayer and penance, solitude and silence.

2. If hermits publicly profess the evangelical counsels before a bishop and live under his direction they are legally accepted as living the consecrated life.

Supplementary Documentation

Const. on the Church: From the God-given seed of the counsels a wonderful and wide-spreading tree has grown up in the field of the Lord, branching out into various forms of religious life lived in solitude or community. (43)

Can. 604, 1. There is also the order of virgins, following Christ more closely, liturgically consecrated by the diocesan bishop, mystically espoused to the Son of God, dedicated to God's service.

2. Virgins may form associations, for greater fidelity and in service of the Church.

Supplementary Documentation

Contemplative Life: With vigilant and maternal care the Church has always watched over virgins consecrated to God, considered by St. Cyprian as "a more illustrious part of Christ's flock." (1)

Consecration to a Life of Virginity: The custom of consecrating women to a life of virginity dates back to the early Church. It led to the institution of a solemn rite constituting the candidate a person set apart, a surpassing sign of the Church's love for Christ, an eschatological image of the world to come and of the glory of the heavenly Bride of Christ. In the rite of consecration the Church reveals its love of virginity, asks for God's grace on those who are consecrated, and prays fervently for an outpouring of the Holy Spirit. (1)

Those who consecrate themselves to chastity under the inspiration of the Holy Spirit do so for more fervent love of Christ and greater freedom in the service of their brothers and sisters.

They are to spend their time in works of penance and of mercy, in apostolic activity and in prayer, in keeping with their state of life and spiritual gifts. . . . (2)

Both nuns and women living in the world may thus consecrate themselves. . . . (3)

Decree on the Rite for the Consecration of Virgins: The rite of consecration of virgins is one of the most precious treasures of the Roman liturgy. Jesus Christ left the great gift of sacred virginity as a heritage to his Spouse. It is for this reason that, from apostolic times, virgins have dedicated their chastity to God, adorning the Mystical Body of Christ and enriching it with a wonderful fruitfulness. (Latin text in AAS 62, [1970], 650)

Can. 605. Only the Holy See can approve new forms of consecrated life. Bishops should help and guide new institutes.

Supplementary Documentation

Mutual Relations: In some regions, one can notice a certain eagerness to found new religious institutes. Those whose responsiblity it is to discern the authenticity of each foundation must, humbly indeed, but objectively and steadily, appraise the prospects of the future and the signs of a possible presence of the Holy Spirit, either to receive his gifts "with thanksgiving and consolation" or to prevent institutes being imprudently brought "into being which are useless or lacking in sufficient resources." In fact, when the judgment relating to the birth of an institute takes into account only the usefulness or expediency of its activity, or when it is based on the activity of a person who shows ambiguous signs of devotion, it is clear that the genuine concept of religious life in the Church is in some ways distorted. (51)

Decree on Religious Life: When it is proposed to found new religious institutes the question must be seriously pondered, whether they are necessary, or even useful, and whether it will be possible for them to grow. (18)

Canonical Commentary

Pope Pius XII gave official approval to secular institutes as an evangelical way of life with his Apostolic Constitution, *Provida Mater Ecclesia*, 2 February, 1947.

Can. 606. The legislation applies equally to men and women, unless the context or the nature of the case indicate otherwise.

Canonical Commentary

The principle of equality between men and women is declared.

Title II: Religious Institutes

Can. 607, 1. Religious life is consecration to God, a marriage established by God, wherein religious complete their self-sacrifice to God, their lives a constant worship of God in charity.

Supplementary Documentation

Exhortation on Religious Life: The teaching of the Council illustrates well the grandeur of this self-giving freely made by yourselves, after the pattern of Christ's self-giving to his Church: like his, yours is total and irreversible. It is precisely for the sake of the kingdom of heaven that you have vowed to Christ, generously and without reservation, that capacity to love, that need to possess, that freedom to regulate your own lives which is so precious to men and women. Such is your consecration, made within the Church and through her ministry. (7)

Can. 607, 2. Members of a religious institute live together and take public vows.

Supplementary Documentation

Contemplative Dimension: The religious community is itself a theological reality, an object of contemplation.

As "a family united in the Lord's name," it is of its nature the place where the experience of God should be able in a special way to come to fullness and be communicated to others.

Acceptance of one another in charity helps to "create an atmosphere favourable to the spiritual progress of each one." (15)

Can. 607, 3. The witness of religious to Christ and the Church implies distancing from the world, in keeping with the institute's purpose.

CHAPTER 1: THE ESTABLISHMENT AND SUPPRESSION OF RELIGIOUS HOUSES

Can. 608. A religious community must live under a superior in a house containing an oratory in which the eucharist is celebrated and reserved, something central to the community.

Supplementary Documentation

Exhortation on Religious Life: Your communities, since they are united in Christ's name, naturally have as their centre the Eucharist, "the sacrament of love, the sign of unity and the bond of charity." It is therefore normal that these communities should be visibly united around an oratory, in which the Eucharist expresses and at the same time makes real that which must be the principal mission of every religious family, as also of every Christian assembly. (48)

Contemplative Dimension: The celebration of the Eucharist and fervent participation in it, "the source and apex of all Christian life" is the irreplaceable, enlivening centre of the contemplative dimension of every religious community.

Priest religious, therefore, should give a pre-eminent place to the daily celebration of the Eucharistic Sacrifice.

Each and every religious should participate actively in the celebration of the Eucharist every day.... "The commitment to participate daily in the Eucharistic sacrifice will help religious to renew their self-offering to the Lord every day. Gathered in the Lord's name, religious communities have the Eucharist as their natural centre. It is normal, therefore, that they should be visibly assembled in their chapel, in which the presence of the Blessed Sacrament expresses and realizes what must be the principal mission of every religious family." (9)

Can. 609, 1, 2. The written permission of the diocesan bishop is required for the establishment of a religious house and, also, for the establishment of a monastery of nuns, of the Holy See.

Canonical Commentary

An institute's constitutions state who is the competent authority in the institute to establish houses. Normally, this is the superior general, who requires the consent of his council.

Can. 610, 1, 2. When establishing a house one must ask if it is useful to Church and institute, conducive to religious life and economically viable.

Can. 611, 1, 2, 3. A bishop's permission to establish a house grants permission to live the religious life, exercise the apostolate and, for a clerical institute, to have a church and exercise the sacred ministry in it.

Supplementary Documentation

Norms on Bishops: Religious are also bound by the laws and decrees laid down in accordance with law by the local ordinary regarding public worship in their churches and public oratories and in their semi-public oratories if the faithful ordinarily attend there, without prejudice however to the right to use its own rite for its community service and while respecting the order of choral divine office and of other sacred functions related to the special purpose of the institute. (26)

Can. 612. Permission of the diocesan bishop is required for a switch to a different kind of apostolic activity, not however for internal changes that merely affect government and discipline.

Canonical Commentary

Such internal changes are those which merely affect the juridical status of the house within the institute.

Can. 613, 1, 2. A religious house of canons regular or of monks, under its own moderator, is *sui juris* and its moderator is a major superior.

Can. 614. Monasteries of nuns associated with a men's institute have their own way of life and government. The association should be to their mutual profit.

Can. 615. Certain monasteries which are *sui juris*, but are not under a major superior other than their own superior, come under the diocesan bishop's special care.

Can. 616, 1, 2, 3, 4. The suppression of a religious house is a matter for the Holy See if it is the only house in the institute or if it is a monastery of nuns and *sui* *juris.* It is a matter for the general chapter if it is a house of canons regular or of monks, otherwise it is a matter for the supreme moderator of the institute. Disposal of the property is for the Holy See to determine in the case of the sole house of an institute, otherwise it is a matter for the constitutions.

CHAPTER 2: GOVERNMENT OF INSTITUTES

ARTICLE 1: SUPERIORS AND COUNCILS.

Can. 617. Superiors should do their job in accordance with law.

Can. 618. Superiors should exercise power in a spirit of service, should be docile to God's will, governing their subjects as God's sons/daughters. They should encourage a spirit of free obedience and co-operation and should listen. They should not however relinquish their own decision-making.

Supplementary Documentation

Decree on Religious Life: Superiors will have to render an account of the souls committed to their care. They should be docile to God's will in performing the task laid upon them and should exercise authority in a spirit of service to the sisters/brothers, thus giving expression to God's love for them.

They should govern their subjects in the realization that they are sons/daughters of God and with respect for them as human persons, fostering in them a spirit of voluntary subjection....They should train their subjects to cooperate with them by applying themselves to their ordinary duties and to new undertakings with an active and responsible obedience. Superiors ought therefore to listen to their subjects willingly and ought to promote cooperation with them for the good of the institute and of the Church, retaining however their own authority to decide and to prescribe what is to be done. (14)

Exhortation on Religious Life: Exercising authority in the midst of your sisters/brothers means therefore being their servants, in accordance with the example of him who gave "his life for a ransom for many" (Matt 20:28). (24)

Consequently, authority and obedience are exercised in the service of the common good as two complementary aspects of the same participation in Christ's offering. For those in authority, it is a matter of serving in their brothers/sisters the design of the Father's love; while in accepting their directives, the religious follow our Master's example and cooperate in the work of salvation. Thus, far from being in opposition to one another, authority and individual liberty go together in the fulfilment of God's will, which is sought in dialogue between the superior and his/her brother/sister, in personal situations, or through a general agreement in what concerns the whole community. (25)

Can. 619. Superiors should take their job seriously, endeavouring to build a community in which God is especially sought and loved, nourishing them frequently with God's word, and seeing to the celebration of the sacred liturgy. They should give an example of virtue and of observance of laws and traditions. They should see to personal needs and should look after the sick, should correct, console, be patient.

Supplementary Documentation

Exhortation on Religious Life: It is the duty of everyone, but especially of superiors and those who exercise responsibility among their brothers or sisters, to awaken in the community the certainties of faith which must be their guide. (25) Does not the heart often let itself cling to what is passing? Many of you will in fact be obliged to lead your lives, at least in part, in a world which tends to exile men and women from themselves and to compromise both their spiritual unity and their union with God. You must therefore learn to find God even under those conditions of life which are marked by an increasingly accelerated rhythm and by noise and the attraction of the ephemeral. (33) Everyone can see how much the fraternal setting of an ordered existence with freely undertaken discipline of life helps you to attain union with God. This discipline is increasingly necessary for anyone who "returns to the heart" (Isaiah 46:8) in the biblical sense of the term, something deeper than our feelings, ideas and wishes, something imbued with the idea of the infinite, the absolute, or eternal destiny. (34)

Can. 620. Among major superiors are numbered those, and their vicars, who govern an institute or a province, abbot primates and superiors of monastic congregations.

Can. 621. A province comprises a number of houses under the same superior.

Can. 622. A supreme moderator has power over all provinces, houses and members, other superiors within their own limits.

Can. 623. A fixed time must have elapsed after perpetual or definitive profession before a person can validly become a superior.

Can. 624, 1. Superiors, though not necessarily superiors general or superiors of houses which are *sui juris*, should hold office for a limited time.

2. An institute's law should ensure that superiors do not hold office for too long a succession of terms.

3. Superiors may be removed from office or transferred.

Can. 625, 1. The supreme moderator of an institute is elected.

2. The bishop presides at elections of superiors of the houses described in Can. 615 and at elections of supreme moderators of institutes of diocesan law.

3. Other superiors are either elected and confirmed by the major superior or appointed after consultation.

Can. 626. Appointments and elections should be in accord with the law, should be done without personal bias, with no other thought than God and the good of the institute and without solicitation of votes.

Canonical Commentary

The purpose of the Canon is to ensure that, all things considered, the most capable person for an office be elected. It does not consider the question of preliminary discussions. Therefore, private or public discussions on the suitability of particular persons for office is neither forbidden nor recommended. The possibility of consultation is often included in constitutions. Charity and justice should be always observed. Public or private discussions should be limited to imparting information on the abilities or limitations of particular persons and on their suitability for the office in question. Persuading or counselling people how to vote is to be avoided.

Can. 627, 1. Superiors should have councils and should avail of their services.

2. An institute's own law should determine when, apart from what the general law lays down, consent of council are required for validity.

Canonical Commentary

Universal and particular law determine when consent of council are required for validity. Consent implies the decisive or deliberative vote of a council. Superiors act invalidly if they act without, or contrary to, the majority vote in a matter where the consent or deliberative vote of the council is required. Counsel, or a consultative vote, means that superiors have to listen to their councils, but the code does not oblige them to follow even the unanimous vote of their councils in such matters. Obviously, superiors would need to have serious reasons for not following such advice.

In matters where counsel or consultation is required, superiors act invalidly if they do not hear their council, according to Can. 127, 2, 1 and 2.

Can. 628, 1. Superiors whose task it is should conduct visitations of houses and members.

2. Diocesan bishops should conduct visitations, even with regard to religious discipline, of (1) monasteries described in Can. 615, (2) houses of institutes of diocesan law in his diocese.

3. Members should be honest with the visitator and nobody has the right to dispense members from this obligation or to obstruct the visitation.

Canonical Commentary

Superiors who are obliged by the constitutions to conduct visitations should do so at the appropriate times. Visitations are conducted by major superiors, their frequency to be determined by the law of each institute. The purpose of a visitation is to promote the proper conduct of the religious life. Abuses and failures in government and administration should be corrected. The visitator should make whatever decisions are necessary to restore, preserve and foster faithful regular observance.

Members of an institute should be open with the visitator and should answer questions truthfully. Visitators may lawfully question members about their personal conduct under the heading of government, but they may not demand or request a manifestation of conscience (Can. 630, 5). They may lawfully enquire about the external conduct of a religious which is knowable to others. A manifestation of conscience involves the revelation of internal acts or of acts which, though external, are not knowable to others. Visitators have the right to use information acquired during visitation in giving instructions or making charges or corrections. However, they may not act on information acquired by manifestation of conscience without the consent of the person concerned.

Nobody should interfere with the purpose of the visitation by commanding or persuading others to conceal the truth in any way.

Can. 629. Superiors should live in their own houses, leaving them only when the law permits.

Canonical Commentary

Superiors should not be absent for prolonged periods, even in the exercise of the ministry.

Can. 630, 1. Superiors should accord due liberty to their subjects with regard to the sacrament of penance and the direction of conscience.

2. Superiors should ensure the availability of suitable confessors for frequent confession.

3. Ordinary confessors should be appointed for monasteries of nuns, houses of formation and larger houses of lay religious, after consultation with the community, with no obligation to confess to go to them.

4. Superiors may not hear subjects' confession, unless requested.

5. Subject should feel able to open their minds to their superiors. Superiors are forbidden to persuade them to manifest their consciences to them.

Canonical Commentary

Neither in 1 nor 2 does the code make frequent confession obligatory, nor does it specify a frequency. With regard to 4, it is to be noted that the ruling that superiors may not hear the confessions of their subjects, unless they freely and spontaneously request it, applies also to novice masters and their assistants, as stipulated in Can. 985. The purpose of the ruling is to avoid any abuse of sacramental knowledge.

With regard to 5, it is to be noted that there is no obligation on subjects to open their minds to superiors. This is only a counsel.

ARTICLE 2: CHAPTERS

Can. 631, 1. The general chapter is the supreme authority in an institute and it should be truly representative. Its task is to safeguard the institute's patrimony as described in Can. 578, to promote renewal and adaptation, to elect the supreme moderator, to deal with matters of greater moment and to issue universally-binding norms.

2. An institute's laws determine the chapter's composition, scope and order of business.

3. Provinces, communities and individuals may send proposals and suggestions to the chapter.

Supplementary Documentation

Decree on Religious Life: Chapters and councils should faithfully discharge the role committed to them in government and, each of them in its own way, should give expression to the involvement and the concern of all the members of the community for the good of the whole. (14)

Norms on Religious Life: It is the institutes themselves which have the main responsibility for renewal and adaptation. They shall accomplish this especially by means of general chapters.... The task of general chapters is not limited to making laws; they should also foster spiritual and apostolic vitality. (1)

The cooperation of all superiors and subjects is necessary for the renewal of their own religious lives, for the preparation of the spirit which should animate the chapters, for the accomplishment of the laws and norms laid down by the chapters. (2)

Can. 632. Each institute must draw up regulations with regard to other chapters.

Can. 633, 1, 2. Participation and consultation should extend to all members and should be wise and sensible.

ARTICLE 3: PROPERTY AND ITS ADMINISTRATION

Can. 634, 1. Institutes, provinces, houses are capable of acquiring, possessing, administering and alienating property.

2. They should however avoid luxury, excessive profit and accumulation of possessions.

Supplementary Documentation

Religious and Human Advancement: The witness of religious for justice in the world implies, especially for them, a constant review of their life-options, of their use of property, of their pattern of relationships. Anybody who has the courage to speak to others of justice must first be seen by them to be just. (4)

The power of transformation which is contained in the spirit of the Beatitudes and penetrates dynamically the life of religious, characterizes their vocation and mission. For them the first and primary liberation is the encounter with Christ, poor among the poor, testifying that they really believe in the preeminence of the kingdom of God above all earthly things and in its highest demands. (19)

Exhortation on Religious Life: In a civilization and a world of almost indefinite material growth, what witness would be offered by religious who let themselves be carried away by an uncurbed seeking for their own ease, and who considered it normal to allow themselves without discernment or restraint everything that is offered them? At a time when there is an increased danger for many of being enticed by the alluring security of possessions, knowledge and power, the call of God places you at the pinnacle of the Christian conscience. You are to remind men and women that their true and complete progress consists in responding to their call "to share as sons and daughters in the life of the living God, the Father of all." (19)

Can. 635, 1. The property of religious institutes is regulated by the provisions of book five of the code.

2. Each institute should have its own regulations, designed to foster and express poverty.

Can. 636, 1. The property of an institute and of a province should be administered by a bursar, under the superior's direction. A major superior may not be bursar and even in houses there should as far as possible be a bursar distinct from the superior.

2. Bursars and other administrators must report on their administration.

Can. 637. The monasteries described in Can. 615 must report annually to the diocesan bishop on their administration. He is also entitled to know about the economic affairs of a house of diocesan law.

Can. 638, 1. An institute's own law must determine the limits to ordinary administration and what belongs to 'extraordinary administration.'

Canonical Commentary

The term 'ordinary administration' covers those activities carried out by administrators in virtue of their office or of delegated authority. It includes whatever is necessary for maintaining and improving church property, collecting interest and rents, paying bills, receiving payments, depositing money in the bank. It also includes what is done at fixed intervals, whether annually or monthly. It has to do with whatever is required for the normal transaction of business, in other words.

Special permission is required, however, for whatever is done by way of 'extraordinary administration.' The term covers matters which do not occur at regular intervals, are of greater importance and exceed the limits of ordinary administration. It includes buying and selling immovable property, borrowing large sums of money, investing money or changing investments, erecting new buildings or making extraordinary repairs. The Canon states that an institute's own law has to determine which matters exceed the scope of ordinary administration. Administrators act invalidly when they exceed the limits and method of ordinary administration, unless they have first obtained permission from the local ordinary (Can. 1281, 1). The normal practice is for an institute's law to determine a certain sum of money which local superiors may spend for extraordinary expenses. Beyond that limit, they are required to have recourse to the higher superior.

Can. 638, 2. Superiors and officials may perform administrative functions validly within their limits.

Canonical Commentary

An institute's laws may require that superiors and officials such as bursars seek the permission of higher authority to perform the more important functions of ordinary administration.

Can. 638, 3. The written permission of the competent superior, with the consent of his/her council is required for alienation of property or for a transaction which diminishes its value. In certain instances the permission of the Holy See is also required.

Canonical Commentary

Strictly speaking, 'alienation' means the transfer of ownership of property, but in the wider sense it also covers giving the use of property to another while retaining ownership. This would include renting, leasing, mortgaging and such like. Alienation therefore means any transaction by which property is transferred to another or is exposed to danger of loss or is withdrawn from direct possession for a considerable length of time. Alienation of Church property is any transaction by which the property is placed in a less favourable condition, so that the rights of the house, province or institute (in the present instance) are less secure. Canon 1291 states that the permission of the competent authority is necessary for the alienation of property which is legitimately part of the 'stable patrimony' of a 'public juridical person' — in this context, a religious house, province, institute. The 'stable patrimony' is what constitutes the basis of the financial security of the body in question. Immovable property, such as houses and lands, is part of 'stable patrimony,' money is not. Free capital is cash on hand, or money temporarily invested or put aside for future needs. Spending money to meet ordinary or extraordinary expenses is not alienation.

The permission of the Holy See is required for the alienation (1) of property the value of which exceeds the limit set for the region, (2) of objects regarded as precious either for artistic reasons, such as sculpture, paintings, etc., or for historical reasons, such as ancient manuscripts, (3) of goods donated to the Church because of a vow.

Alienation of property also requires (1) that there be a just cause, such as urgent necessity, evident utility, piety, charity or any other grave pastoral reason, (2) a written estimate by experts, (3) any other precautions prescribed by legitimate authority. All this in order to prevent a loss. (Can. 1293, 1, 2.)

Normally a property or object should not be disposed of for less than its value and the money paid should be used wisely for the good of the house, province or institute, or should be prudently invested — depending on the purpose for which the property was sold.

Can. 638, 4. The monasteries described in Can. 615 and institutes of diocesan law need the written consent of the diocesan bishop, for alienation of property.

Can. 639, 1. A juridical person is answerable for debts incurred by itself.

2. An individual member is liable for debts on his/her own behalf with permission, but the institute is liable when the individual is acting on its instructions and on its behalf.

3. The individual member is liable if acting without permission.

4. An action can be taken against the person who has profited from the transaction.

5. Religious superiors must not incur debts unless they can pay the interest from normal resources and repay the capital in a reasonable time.

Can. 640. Institutes should give a collective witness to charity and poverty by contributing to the needs of the Church and of the poor.

Supplementary Documentation

Exhortation on Religious Life: . . . religious institutes have an important role to fulfil in the sphere of works of mercy, assistance and social justice; it is clear that in carrying out this service they must always be attentive to the call of the gospel. (16)

You hear rising up, more pressing than ever, from their personal distress and collective misery, "the cry of the poor." Was it not in order to respond to their appeal as God's privileged ones that Christ came, even going so far as to identify himself with them? In a world experiencing the full flood of development this persistence of poverty-stricken masses and individuals constitutes a pressing call for a conversion of minds and attitudes, especially for you who follow Christ more closely in this earthly condition of self-emptying. (17)

Religious and Human Advancement: The many works and activities which, with their various charisms, are characteristic of the apostolate of religious are among the most important vehicles for the Church's mission of evangelization and human advancement. (5)

Canonical Commentary

Canon 1285 states that within the limits of ordinary administration it is permissible for administrators of movable goods which do not form part of a 'stable patrimony' to make donations to charity. Canon 1286 prescribes that with regard to employees the civil laws which regulate labour relations and social life should be adhered to, in accordance with the Church's teaching; that employees be paid a just salary which will enable them and their families to develop their religious, family, social and cultural lives adequately. Canon 1265 states that, the right of mendicants apart, the written permission of their own bishop and of the bishop of the place is required for the collection of offerings for any pious or ecclesiastical institute; that the conference of bishops can issue regulations concerning the collection of alms, regulations binding on all.

CHAPTER 3: THE ADMISSION OF CANDIDATES AND THE FORMATION OF MEMBERS

ARTICLE 1: ADMISSION TO THE NOVITIATE

Can. 641. Admission of candidates is for the major superior.

Canonical Commentary

There is no mention of postulancy here. The general principle is however stated in Can. 597, 2, which says that nobody should be admitted without proper preparation.

Can. 642. Superiors may admit only those with the required age, health, character and maturity. Expert advice may be sought.

Supplementary Documentation

Instruction on Renewal: Superiors responsible for the admission of candidates to the novitiate will take care to accept only those giving proof of the aptitudes and elements of maturity regarded as necessary for commitment to the religious life as lived in the institute. (14)

Canonical Commentary

While it is accepted that experts may be consulted, if necessary, there is a reminder of the prohibition in Can. 220 of violation of a person's privacy. While psychological tests may be deemed necessary, there is an obvious warning against abuses in this matter if tests are imposed unnecessarily and against a person's will.

Can. 643, 1. If any of the following are admitted, their admission is invalid: a person under seventeen, a married person, a member (not just a postulant or novice) of another institute, whether this is known or the person conceals it, a person induced by force, grave fear or deceit or whom the superior is similarly induced to accept.

2. An institute can add its own criteria.

Canonical Commentary

An institute can add its own 'impediments to validity,' that is, factors which render admission null and void. It can also add what are called 'conditions.' These are presumed to refer to liceity, that is to say, conditions whose absence makes the admission illicit, but not invalid.

Can. 644. Diocesan clerics may not be admitted without consulting their bishops, nor may the seriously insolvent.

Can. 645, 1. Candidates must provide evidence that they have been baptized, confirmed and are free.

2. Clerics, people who have been in another institute or a seminary, all require appropriate references.

3, 4. Institutes may in their own laws require further evidence and superiors may request further information.

ARTICLE 2: THE NOVITIATE AND THE FORMATION OF NOVICES

Can. 646. The purpose of the novitiate is to deepen the novices' understanding of their calling, to enable them to experience the life of the institute and be formed in its spirit.

Supplementary Documentation

Instruction on Renewal: Religious life begins with the novitiate. Whatever may be the special aim of the institute, the principal purpose of the novitiate is to initiate the novice into the essential and primary requirements of the religious life and, also, in view of a greater charity, to implement the evangelical counsels of chastity, poverty and obedience of which he/she will later make profession, "with the help of vows or other sacred obligations which resemble vows in their nature."

In those institutes where "apostolic and charitable works are essential to the religious life" the novices are to be gradually trained to dedicate themselves to activities in keeping with the purpose of their institute, while developing that intimate union with Christ whence all their apostolic activity must flow. (13)

Can. 647, 1. The establishment, transfer or suppression of a novitiate is a matter for the supreme moderator.

2. Noviceship must be passed in a novitiate, but the supreme moderator may permit individual exceptions.

3. The major superior may transfer the novices to another house.

Supplementary Documentation

Instruction on Renewal: The erection of a novitiate does not require the authorization of the Holy See. It belongs to the superior general, with the consent of his council and conformably to the norms laid down in the constitutions, to erect or to authorize the erection of a novitiate, to determine the special details of the program and to decide on its location in a given house of the Institute.

If necessary, in order to make more effective provision for the formation of the novices, the superior general may authorize the transfer of the novitiate community during certain periods to another residence designated by himself. (16)

In case of necessity, the superior general, with the consent of his council and after consultation with the interested provincial, may authorize the erection of several novitiates within the same province. (17)

In view of the very important role of community life in the formation of the novices, and when the small number of the novices would prevent the creation of conditions favorable to genuine community life, the superior general should, if possible, organize the novitiate in another community of the Institute able to assist in the formation of this small group of novices. (18)

In special cases and by way of exception, the superior general, with the consent of his council, is empowered to allow a candidate to make his novitiate validly in some house of the Institute other than the novitiate, under the responsibility of an experienced religious acting as novice master. (19)

Can. 648, 1, 2, 3. Noviceship lasts a minimum of twelve months to a maximum of two years, with periods of apostolic work being permitted in between.

Can. 649, 1. Absences from the novitiate house, other than those envisaged in the two preceding Canons, of between a fortnight and three months have to be made up later; an absence of more than three months makes the noviceship invalid.

2. First profession may be advanced by a fortnight.

Supplementary Documentation

Exhortation on Renewal: In order to be valid, the novitiate must last twelve months. (21)

Absences from the novitiate group and house which, either at intervals or continuously, exceed three months render the novitiate invalid.

As for absences lasting less than three months, it pertains to the major superiors, after consultation with the novice master, to decide in each individual case, taking into account the reasons for the absence, whether this absence should be made up by demanding an extension of the novitiate, and to determine the length of the eventual prolongation. The constitutions of the institution may provide directives on this point. (22)

The general chapter, by at least a two-thirds majority, may decide, on an experimental basis, to integrate into novitiate formation one or several periods involving activities in line with the character of the Institute and away from the novitiate, in the degree in which, in the judgment of the novice master and with the consent of the major superior, such an experiment would seem to be a useful contribution to formation.

These formation stages may be used for one or several novices or for the novitiate community as a whole. Wherever possible, it would be preferable that the novices take part in these stages in groups of two or more.

During these stages away from the novitiate community, the novices remain under the responsibility of the novice master. (23)

The total length of the periods spent by a novice outside the novitiate will be added to the twelve months of presence required by no. 21 for the validity of the novitiate, but in such a way that the total duration of the novitiate thus expanded does not exceed two years.

These formative apostolic periods may not begin until after a minimum of three months in the novitiate and will be distributed in such a way that the novice will spend at least six continuous months in the novitiate and return to the novitiate for at least one month prior to first vows or temporary commitment.

In cases where superiors would deem it useful for a future novice to have a period of experience before beginning the three months of presence required at the start of the novitiate, this period could be regarded as a probation period and only after its completion would the novitiate begin. (24)

The nature of experimental periods outside the novitiate can vary according to the aims of various institutes and the nature of their activities. Still, they must always be planned and carried out in view of forming the novice or, in certain cases, testing his aptitude for the life of the institute. Besides gradual preparation for apostolic activities, they can also have as their purpose to bring the novice into contact with certain concrete aspects of poverty or of labour, to contribute to character formation, a better knowledge of human nature, the strengthening of the will, the development of personal responsibility and, lastly, to provide occasions for effort at union with God in the context of the active life.

This balancing of periods of activity and periods of retreat consecrated to prayer, meditation or study, which will characterize the formation of the novices, should stimulate them to remain faithful to it through the whole of their religious life. It would also be well for such period of retreat to be regularly planned during the years of formation preceding perpetual profession. (25)

The major superior may, for a just cause, allow first profession to be anticipated, but not beyond fifteen days. (26)

Can. 650, 1. The formation of novices is to be entrusted to a novice master/mistress.

2. The novice master/mistress alone governs the novices, under the major superior.

Supplementary Documentation

Instruction on Renewal: All tasks and work entrusted to novices will be under the responsibility and direction of the novice master/mistress, who nevertheless may seek the aid of competent persons. The chief aim of these various tasks must be the formation of the novices, not the interests of the Congregation. (30)

Unity of heart and mind must reign between superiors, the novice master/mistress and the novices. This union, which is the fruit of genuine charity, is necessary for religious formation.

Superiors and the novice master/mistress must always show towards the novices evangelical simplicity, kindness coupled with gentleness and respect for their personality, in order to build up a climate of confidence, docility and openness in which the novice master / mistress will be able to orientate their generosity toward a complete gift of themselves to the Lord in faith, and gradually lead them by word and example to learn in the mystery of Christ crucified the exigencies of authentic religious obedience. Thus, let the novice master/mistress teach his/her novices 'that the obedience with

which they fulfil their duties and perform their tasks
allotted them is active and responsible.' (32)

Canonical Commentary

The responsibility of the novice master/mistress
cannot be vested in a group of directors *en bloc*, nor is
collegiate government by a group of directors
acceptable.

Can. 651, 1. The novice master/mistress must be perpetually professed.

2. He/she may have assistants.

3. He/she must be well trained and must not be
distracted by other work.

Canonical Commentary

An institute may prescribe other qualifications in
addition to those listed above.

Can. 652, 1. It is for the novice master/mistress to
evaluate the novices' vocations and to form them in the
way of life of the institute.

2. The novices are to be trained in virtue, in prayer
and self-denial, in meditating on the scriptures, in
liturgy, in the observance of the counsels, in the spirit
of the institute, its history and are to be imbued with
love of the Church and of its pastors.

Supplementary Documentation

Instruction on Renewal: The programme as well as the nature of the activities and work of the novitiate must be organised in such a way as to contribute to novice formation.

This formation, confortable to the teaching of the Lord in the Gospel and the demands of the particular aim and spirituality of the institute, consists mainly in initiating the novices gradually into detachment from everything not connected with the kingdom of God, the practice of obedience, poverty, prayer, habitual union with God in availability to the Holy Spirit, in order to help one another in frank and open charity.

The novitiate will also include study and meditation on Holy Scripture, the doctrinal and spiritual formation indispensable for the development of a supernatural life of union with God and an understanding of the religious state and, lastly, an initiation into liturgical life and the spirituality proper to the institute. (15)

In the direction of the novices, particularly during the periods of formative activity, the novice master/mistress will base his/her direction on the teaching so clearly enunciated by the Second Vatican Council: 'In order, therefore, that members may respond to their call to follow Christ above all and to serve Christ himself in his members, their apostolic activities must stem from an intimate union with him.'

'And so members of any religious institute must seek God alone and above all else; they should combine contemplation, by which they become united to him in mind and heart, with apostolic love by which they strive to join in the work of the redemption and spread the kingdom of God.'

With this in mind he/she should teach the novices:

(a) to seek in all things, as well in apostolic activities or the service of men as in the times consecrated to silent prayer or study, purity of intention and the unity of charity towards God and towards men;

(b) when the apostolic activities of their institute lead them to become involved in human affairs, to learn how to use this world as though not using it;

(c) to understand the limitations of their own activity without being discouraged and to work at the ordering of their own life, bearing in mind that no one can give himself authentically to God and his brethren without first getting possession of himself in humility;

(d) to bring about in their lives, along with a will which is firm and rich in initiative, and conformable to the demands of a vocation to an institute dedicated to the apostolate, the indispensable balance on both the human and the supernatural level between times consecrated to the apostolate and the service of men and more or less lengthy periods, in solitude or in community, devoted to prayer and meditative reading of the Word of God;

(e) in fidelity to this program which is essential to every consecrated life, to ground their hearts gradually in union with God and that peace which comes from doing the divine will, whose demands they will have learned to discover in the duties of their state and in the promptings of justice and charity. (31)

Can. 653, 1. A novice may leave or be dismissed.

Canonical Commentary

Superiors will normally encourage a novice to leave before resorting to dismissal. It is presumed that superiors will not want to dismiss a novice without a just reason.

Can. 653, 2. After a novitiate, a novice must be professed temporarily, sent away or have the novitiate prolonged in case of doubt.

Canonical Commentary

The provision whereby a novitiate may be prolonged by the major superior applies also to institutes which have two years novitiate.

ARTICLE 3: RELIGIOUS PROFESSION

Can. 654. In publicly vowing observance of the evangelical counsels religious are consecrated to God by the Church and become members of an institute, with rights and obligations.

Canonical Commentary

A vow is 'public' when it is received in the name of the Church by a legitimate superior (Can. 1192, 1). No distinction is made in this Canon between solemn and simple vows, but Can. 1192, 2, states that a vow is 'solemn' if it is recognised as such by the Church, otherwise it is 'simple.' A public perpetual vow of chastity is now a 'diriment impediment' to marriage, that is to say, it would render an attempted marriage invalid (Can. 1088). The rights and obligations which people acquire when they become members of an institute are defined by law. In religious institutes, temporary commitment must be undertaken by vow.

Can. 655. Temporary profession lasts from three to six years.

Can. 656. For temporary profession to be valid, it must be undertaken after a novitiate, by someone at least eighteen years old, whom the competent superior has decided to admit, after a vote by his/her council, it must be explicit and not consequent on compulsion, grave fear or deceit, it must be accepted by the legitimate superior.

Can. 657, 1. The period of temporary profession is followed by renewal of temporary profession, by perpetual profession, or the person may leave.

2. The competent superior may prolong the period of temporary profession up to a maximum of nine years.

Supplementary Documentation

Instruction on Renewal: In order then to respond to the need for gradual formation the question has arisen concerning the extension of the period prior to perpetual profession in which a candidate is bound by temporary vows or by some other form of commitment.

It is proper that when he pronounces his perpetual vows, the religious should have reached the degree of spiritual maturity required in order that the religious state to which he is committing himself in stable and certain fashion may really be for him a means of perfection and greater love, rather than a burden too heavy to carry. Nevertheless, in certain cases the extension of temporary probation can be an aid to this maturity, while in others it can involve drawbacks which it will not be out of place to point out. The fact of remaining for too long a time in a state of uncertainty is not always a contribution to maturity, and this situation may in some cases encourage a tendency to instability. It should be added that in the case of non-admission to perpetual profession, the return to lay life will often entail problems of readjustment, which will be all the more serious and trying according as the time spent in temporary commitment has been longer. Superiors, consequently, must be aware of their grave responsibilities in this field and should not put off until the last minute a decision which could and should have been taken earlier. (6)

Can. 657, 3. Perpetual profession may be brought forward by up to three months.

Can. 658, 1, 2. To be validly perpetually professed, a person must be over twenty-one and must normally (see above) have been temporarily professed for at least three years. See also Can. 656.

ARTICLE 4: THE FORMATION OF RELIGIOUS

Can. 659, 1. The formation of members in their institute's way of life and mission is to be completed after first profession.

2. An institute's law must prescribe the details, with an eye to the Church's needs and the human condition.

Can. 660, 1. The formation should be spiritual and apostolic, doctrinal and practical, leading to academic degrees where appropriate.

2. Members should not be given work likely to interfere with their studies.

Can. 661. Religious should continue their spiritual, doctrinal and practical formation all their lives and superiors should allow time and should help.

Supplementary Documentation

Decree on Religious Life: The up-to-date renewal of institutes depends very much on the training of the members. For this reason, non-clerical religious men, and religious women, should not be assigned to apostolic tasks immediately after the novitiate. Their religious, apostolic, doctrinal and technical training should, rather, be continued, as is deemed appropriate, in suitable establishments. They should also acquire whatever degrees they need.

Lest adaptation of religious life to the needs of our time be merely external and lest those whose rule assigns them to the active ministry should prove unequal to the task, they should be properly instructed — each according to his/her intellectual calibre and personal bent — concerning the behavior-patterns, the emotional attitudes, and the thought-processes of modern society. The elements of the education should be so harmoniously fused that it will help to integrate the lives of the religious.

All through their lives, religious should endeavor assiduously to perfect this spiritual, doctrinal and technical culture. Superiors, as far as they are able, should provide for them the opportunity, assistance and the time for this.

It is also the task of superiors to see to it that directors, spiritual masters/mistresses and professors are chosen to best advantage and are carefully trained. (18)

Norms on Religious Life: The formation of religious from the novitiate onwards need not be planned according to the same pattern for all institutes, but account must be taken of the specific character of each institute. In revising and adapting this formation, a sufficient measure of prudent experimentation should take place. (33)

What is stated in the Decree *Optatam totius* (On Priestly Formation) must be carefully observed in the formation of religious clerics, with the necessary adaptations demanded by the particular character of each institute. (34)

Post-novitiate formation, adapted to the character of each institute, is absolutely necessary for all subjects, not excepting contemplatives. For institutes of brothers and for the sisters in institutes dedicated to apostolic work, the formation must normally cover the entire period of temporary vows, as is the case already in many institutes, under the name of juniorate or scholasticate or similar terms. (35)

This formation must be given in houses which are suitable for the purpose. It must not be merely theoretical but should be also practical, involving, for their educational value, various activities and duties which fit in with the character and circumstances of each institute. Thus the candidates will be gradually introduced to the kind of life that later on shall be theirs. (36)

Due regard must be had for the kind of training which is proper to the individual institute. But, since all institutes are not able to impart in a satisfactory manner a doctrinal and technical formation, they can make up for this by fraternal collaboration. This can be done on a variety of levels and can assume different forms: lectures or courses in common, the lending of teachers, even by pooling teachers and resources in a common school attended by members of several institutes.

The institutes which are well-provided as regards means of training should be willing to help other institutes. (37)

After a due measure of experimentation, each institute must draw up proper and suitable rules for the training of its subjects. (38)

Decree on Religious Life: Institutes should see to it that their members have a proper understanding of men, of the conditions of the times and of the needs of the Church, this to the end that, making wise judgments about the contemporary world in the light of faith, and burning with apostolic zeal, they may be able to help men more effectively. (2)

CHAPTER 4: OBLIGATIONS AND RIGHTS OF MEMBERS

Can. 662. The following of Christ is the supreme rule of life.

Supplementary Documentation

Decree on Religious Life: Since the final norm of the religious life is the following of Christ as it is put before us in the Gospel, this must be taken by all institutes as the supreme rule.

Before all else, religious life is ordered to the following of Christ by its members and to their becoming united with God by the profession of the evangelical counsels. For this reason, it must be seriously and carefully considered that even the best-contrived adaptations to the needs of our time will be of no avail unless they are animated by a spiritual renewal, which must always be assigned primary importance even in the active ministry. (2)

Religious, therefore, faithful to their profession and leaving all things for Christ's sake (cf. Mk 10:28), should follow him, regarding this as the one thing that is necessary (cf. Lk 10:39) and should be solicitous for all that is his (cf. Cor 7:32) (5)...all those who are called by God to the practice of the evangelical counsels, and who make faithful profession of them, bind themselves to the Lord in a special way. They follow Christ who, virginal and poor (cf. Mt 8:20; Lk 9:58), redeemed and sanctified men by obedience unto death on the cross (cf. Phil 2:8). Under the impulse of love, which the Holy Spirit pours into their hearts (cf. Rom 5:5), they live more and more for Christ and for his Body, the Church (cf. Col 1:24). The more fervently, therefore, they join themselves to Christ by this gift of their whole life, the fuller does the Church's life become and the more vigorous and fruitful its apostolate. (1)

Can. 663, 1. Contemplation and constant prayer are the first and main duty of religious.

2. Members should participate daily in the eucharist, should receive communion and should worship the Lord in the sacrament.

3. They should read the scriptures, practice mental prayer and celebrate the divine office, to which clerics are obliged (Can. 276, 2, 3).

4. They should be devoted to our Lady and the rosary.

5. They should make an annual retreat.

Supplementary Documentation

Contemplative Dimension: The contemplative dimension is basically a reality of grace, experienced by the believer as God's gift. It enables persons to know the Father (cf. Jn 14:8) in the mystery of trinitarian communion (cf. 1 Jn 1-3), so that they can savour *the depths of God* (1 Cor 2:10).

It is not the intention here to discuss the many and delicate problems concerning the different methods of contemplation, nor to analyze contemplation in so far as it is an infused gift of the Holy Spirit.

We describe the contemplative dimension fundamentally as the theological response of faith, hope and charity, by which the believer opens up to the revelation of the living God and to communion with him through Christ in the Holy Spirit. 'The concentration of one's mind and of one's heart on God, which we define as contemplation, becomes the highest and fullest activity of the spirit, the activity which today, also, can and must order the immense pyramid of all human activities'.

As the unifying act of all human movement towards God, the contemplative dimension is expressed by listening to and meditating on the Word of God; by participating in the divine life transmitted to us in the sacraments, particularly the Eucharist; by liturgical and personal prayer; by the constant desire and search for God and for his Will in events and people; by the conscious participation in his salvific mission; by self-giving to others for the coming of the Kingdom. There results, in the religious, an attitude of continuous and humble adoration of God's mysterious presence in people, events and things: an attitude which manifests the virtue of piety, an interior fount of peace and a bearer of peace to every sphere of life and apostolate.

All this is achieved in continual purification of heart under the light and guidance of the Holy Spirit, so that we can find God in all things and people and become the 'praise of his glory' (Eph 1:6).

The very nature of consecrated life stands out in this way as the profound source which nourishes and unifies every aspect of the lives of religious. (1)

Prayer is the indispensible breath of every contemplative dimension. In these times of apostolic renewal, as always in every form of missionary engagement, a privileged place is given to contemplation of God, to meditation on his plan of salvation, and to reflection on the signs of the times in the light of the Gospel, so that prayer may be nourished and grow in quality and frequency'. In this way, prayer, open to creation and history, becomes acknowledgement, adoration and constant praise of the presence of God in the world and its history and the echo of a life of solidarity with one's brothers and sisters, especially the poor and the suffering.

This prayer, personal and community, will come about only if the hearts of religious reach a high level of vitality and intensity in dialogue with God and in union with Christ, Redeemer of humanity. Therefore, in the sometimes exhausting rhythm of apostolic commitments, there must be well-ordered and sufficiently prolonged daily and weekly periods of personal and community prayer. There must also be more intensive moments of recollection and prayer every month and throughout the year.

Decree on Religious Life: The members of each institute ought to seek God before all else, and solely; they should join contemplation, by which they cleave to God by mind and heart, to apostolic love, by which they endeavor to be associated with the work of redemption and to spread the kingdom of God.

They who make profession of the evangelical counsels should seek and love above all else God who has first loved us (cf. 1 Jn 4:10). In all circumstances they should take care to foster a life hidden with Christ in God (cf. Col 3:3), which is the source and stimulus of love of the neighbor, for the salvation of the world and the building-up of the Church. Even the very practice of the evangelical counsels is animated and governed by this charity.

For this reason, members of institutes should assiduously cultivate the spirit of prayer and prayer itself, drawing on the authentic sources of Christian spirituality. In the first place, let them have the sacred scripture at hand daily, so that they might learn "the surpassing worth of knowing Christ Jesus" (Phil 3:8) by reading and meditating on the divine scriptures. They should perform the sacred liturgy, especially the holy mystery of the Eucharist, with their hearts and their lips, according to the mind of the Church, and they should nourish their spiritual lives from this richest of sources.

Thus, refreshed at the table of the divine law and of the sacred altar, let them love the members of Christ as brothers, let them reverence and love their pastors in a filial spirit; let them more and more live and think with the Church, and let them dedicate themselves wholeheartedly to its mission. (5,6)

Exhortation on Renewal: Finally, there is surely no need to remind you of the special place occupied in your community life by the Church's liturgy, the center of which is the Eucharistic Sacrifice, in which interior prayer is linked to external worship. At the moment of your religious profession you were offered to God by the Church in close union with the Eucharistic Sacrifice. Day after day this offering of yourselves must become a reality, concretely and continuously renewed. Communion in the Body and Blood of Christ is the primary source of this renewal; by it may your will to love truly, and even to the sacrifice of your lives, be unceasingly confirmed. (47)

Norms on Religious Life: The study and meditation of the Gospel and of the whole of Holy Scripture by all religious, from the time of the novitiate, should be more strongly encouraged. Further, care should be taken that all of them share, in whatever ways are most suitable, in the mystery and life of the Church. (15)

Contemplative Dimension: The celebration of the Eucharist and fervent participation in it, 'the source and apex of all christian life,' is the irreplaceable, enlivening centre of the contemplative dimension of every religious community.

Priest religious, therefore, will give a pre-eminent place to the daily celebration of the Eucharistic Sacrifice.

Each and every religious should take an active part in it every day according to the concrete circumstances in which their community lives and works. 'That more perfect participation is highly recommended, by which the faithful, after the priest's communion, receive the Body of the Lord from the same Sacrifice.'

'The commitment to take part daily in the Eucharistic Sacrifice will help religious to renew their self-offering to the Lord every day. Gathered in the Lord's name, religious communities have the Eucharist as their natural centre. It is normal, therefore, that they should be visibly assembled in their chapel, in which the presence of the Blessed Sacrament expresses and realizes what must be the principal mission of every religious family.'

'The Divine Office, in that it is the public prayer of the Church, is a source of devotion and nourishment for personal prayer.' It is 'designed to sanctify the whole course of the day.'

The willingness with which religious communities have already responded to the Church's exhortation to the faithful of all walks of life to celebrate the divine praises shows how much they appreciate the importance of this more intimate participation in the Church's life.

The contemplative dimension of the lives of religious will find constant inspiration and nourishment in the measure that they dedicate themselves to the Office with attention and fidelity. A greater appreciation of the spiritual riches in the Office of Readings could also help achieve this.

The Virgin Mary is a model for every consecrated person and for participation in the apostolic mission of the Church. This is particularly evident when we consider the spiritual attitudes which characterized her:

The Virgin Mary listening to the Word of God;

The Virgin Mary at prayer — 'a most excellent model of the Church in the order of faith, charity, and perfect union with Christ, that is, of that interior disposition with which the Church, beloved spouse, is closely associated with her Lord, invokes him and through him, worships the Eternal Father';

The Virgin Mary standing courageously by the Cross of the Lord and teaching us contemplation of the Passion.

By reviving devotion to her, according to the teaching and tradition of the Church, religious will find the sure way to illuminate and strengthen the contemplative dimension of their lives.

'The contemplative life of religious would be incomplete if it were not directed in filial love towards her who is the Mother of the Church and of consecrated souls. This love for the Virgin will be manifested with the celebration of her feasts and, in particular, with daily prayer in her honour, especially the Rosary. The daily recitation of the Rosary is a centuries old tradition for religious, and so it is not out of place to recall the suitability, beauty and efficacy of this prayer, which proposes for our meditation the mysteries of the Lord's life.' (13)

Can. 664. Religious should examine their conscience daily and receive the sacrament of penance frequently.

Supplementary Documentation

Decree on Confession for Religious: The Church is 'continually engaged in repentance and renewal' and religious, because of their special union with the Church, should value highly the sacrament of Penance. The sacrament of Penance restores and strengthens in members of the Church who have sinned the fundamental gift of 'metanoia,' of conversion to the kingdom of Christ, which is first received in Baptism. Those who approach this sacrament receive from God's mercy the pardon of their offenses and at the same time they are reconciled to the Church which they have wounded by their sins.

Religious should likewise hold in high esteem the frequent use of this sacrament. It is a practice which increases true knowledge of one's self, favors Christian humility and offers the occasion for salutary spiritual direction and the increase of grace. These and other wonderful effects not only contribute greatly to daily and more rapid growth in virtue, but are likely beneficial to the common good of the whole community. (2) (Text in Flannery)

Contemplative Dimension: The Sacrament of Reconciliation which 'restores and revives the fundamental gift of conversion received in Baptism' has a particularly important function for growth in the spiritual life. There can be no contemplative dimension without a personal and community experience of conversion.

The Fathers of the congregation for Religious and Secular Institutes again appeal for:

An appropriate and regular personal reception of this Sacrament;

The ecclesial and fraternal dimension which is made more evident when this Sacrament is celebrated with a community rite, while the confession remains always a personal act.

Can. 665, 1. Religious must live in common, leaving their house only with permission. The major superior may grant permission for a longer absence, but there has to be a special reason for an absence of longer than one year.

2. A religious who has run away should be persuaded to return.

Can. 666. Religious should avoid whatever in the media might endanger their vocation or their chastity.

Can. 667, 1. There should be a cloister in every house and a portion of the house reserved to the religious.

2. There is to be a stricter cloister in contemplative monasteries.

3. Monasteries of totally contemplative nuns must have papal cloister, other monasteries of nuns a cloister in keeping with their nature.

4. A diocesan bishop may enter a monastery of nuns in his diocese, may allow others to enter it, with the superior's permission, and nuns to go out.

Supplementary Documentation

Decree on Religious Life: Papal cloister is to be maintained for nuns whose life is wholly contemplative. However, it should be adjusted to suit the conditions of time and place, abolishing obsolete practices after consultation with the monasteries themselves. Other nuns, however, who are engaged in the external apostolate by virtue of their own rule are to be exempted from papal cloister so that they can the better fulfil their apostolic tasks. The cloister prescribed by the constitutions must be maintained, however.

Norms on Religious Life: The papal enclosure of monasteries must be considered as an ascetical institution which is singularly appropriate to the particular vocation of nuns, and as one which stands as a sign and a protection; it is the particular form which their withdrawal from the world takes.

In the same manner, nuns of the Eastern Church must keep their enclosure. (30)

This enclosure must be so adapted that the material separation from the outside world is always preserved. The individual religious families are left free, in pursuance of their own spirit, to set out and define in their constitutions the particular norms of the material separation. (31)

The minor enclosure is suppressed. Those nuns who from their institution are dedicated to external activities, must define their enclosure in their constitutions. But those nuns who, though contemplative from their institution have adopted external works, must, after a suitable space of time left to them for deliberation, either abandon external works and retain papal enclosure, or maintain these activities and define the nature of their enclosure in their constitutions, while still remaining nuns. (32)

Instruction on Contemplative Life: The enclosure reserved for nuns totally dedicated to contemplation is called papal since the norms which govern it must be sanctioned by apostolic authority, even though they are established by particular law, by which are fitly expressed the characteristics proper to each Institute. (1)

The law of papal enclosure applies to all that part of the house inhabited by the nuns, together with the gardens and orchards, access to which is reserved to the nuns themselves. (2)

The area of the convent subject to the law of enclosure must be circumscribed in such a way that material separation be ensured, that is, all coming in and going out must be thereby rendered impossible (e.g., by a wall or some other effective means, such as a fence of planks or heavy iron mesh, or a thick and firmly rooted hedge). Only through doors kept regularly locked may one enter or leave the enclosure. (3)

The mode of ensuring this effective separation, especially as far as the choir and parlor are concerned, is to be specified in the Constitutions and in supplementary legislative documents, particular consideration being given to the diversity of each Institute's traditions and to the various circumstances of time and place (e.g., grates, lattice-work, stationary partitions, etc.). In conformity with Article 1, however, the means of separation mentioned above must be previously submitted for the approval of the Sacred Congregation for Religious and for Secular Institues. (4)

In virtue of the law of enclosure, the nuns, novices and postulants must live within the confines of the convent prescribed by the enclosure itself, nor may they licitly go beyond them, except in the cases provided for by law. (5)

The law of enclosure likewise forbids anyone, of whatever class, condition, sex or age, to enter the cloistered area of the convent, except in the cases provided for by law. (6)

Can. 668, 1. Individuals must surrender administration of their property before first profession and must make their will before perpetual profession.

2. They need the superior's permission to change these arrangements or to do anything with property.

3. Their earnings, pension, subvention or insurance go to the institute, unless otherwise determined.

4. Whether an institute demands total renunciation of property or permits total or partial renunciation, this must be done at final profession.

5. Where total renunciation is the norm, religious forfeit all right to possess or acquire property.

Can. 669, 1, 2. Religious must wear a habit, clerical members of an institute without a habit must wear clerical dress.

✓ *Supplementary Documentation*

Decree on Religious Life: The religious habit, as a symbol of consecration, must be simple and modest, at once poor and becoming. In addition, it must be in keeping with the requirements of health and it must be suited to the times and place and to the needs of the apostolate. The habits, both of men and of women, which are not in conformity with these norms ought to be changed. (17)

Norms on Bishops: [Religious are bound by] laws, decrees and ordinance of the local ordinary or of the conference of bishops which. . . deal with: (d) ecclesiastical dress, in accordance with the following rule: the local ordinary or the episcopal conference to prevent scandal to the faithful can prohibit clerics, both secular and religious, even exempt religious, from wearing lay dress in public.

Can. 670. The institute must supply the needs of the religious.

Can. 671. A religious needs permission to do outside work.

Can. 672. Religious are bound to celibacy (Can. 277), are forbidden to do anything unbecoming or foreign to the clerical state, to take public office in government, to take on the management of the property of lay people, to go bail, sign bonds, though members of some lay institutes may get permission (Can. 285); they are forbidden to engage in commerce without permission (Can. 286). Normally, they may not take an active part in party politics or trade unions (Can. 287) and may not voluntarily undertake military service (Can. 289). After their ordination, religious priests must improve their knowledge of the sacred sciences and of pastoral method by attending courses and conferences, etc.

CHAPTER 5: INSTITUTES' APOSTOLATE

Can. 673. The apostolate of all religious is, firstly, the witness of their consecrated life.

Supplementary Documentation

Exhortation on Renewal: The evangelical witness of the religious life clearly manifests to men the primacy of the love of God; it does this with a force for which we must give thanks to the Holy Spirit. In all simplicity — following the example given by our venerated predecessor, John XXIII, on the eve of the Council — we would like to tell you what hope is stirred up in us, as well as in all pastors and faithful of the Church, by the spiritual generosity of those men and women who have consecrated their lives to the Lord in the spirit and practice of the evangelical counsels. We wish also to assist you to continue in your path of following Christ in faithfulness to the Council's teaching. (1)

From the beginning, the tradition of the Church — is it perhaps necessary to recall it? — presents us with this privileged witness of a constant seeking of God, of an undivided love for Christ alone, and of an absolute dedication to the growth of his kingdom. Without this concrete sign there would be a danger that the charity which animates the entire Church would grow cold, that the salvific paradox of the Gospel would be blunted, and that the "salt" of faith would lose its savor in a world undergoing secularization.

From the first centuries, the Holy Spirit has stirred up, side by side with the heroic confession of the martyrs, the wonderful strength of disciples and virgins, of hermits and anchorites. Religious life already existed in germ, and progressively it felt the growing need of developing and of taking on different forms of community or solitary life, in order to respond to the pressing invitation of Christ: "There is no one who has left house, wife, brothers, parents or children for the sake of the kingdom of God who will not be given repayment many times over in this present time, and in the world to come, eternal life."

"Who would venture to hold that such a calling today no longer has the same value and vigor? That the Church could do without these exceptional witnesses of the transcendence of the love of Christ? Or that the world without damage to itself could allow these lights to go out? They are lights which announce the kingdom of God with a liberty which knows no obstacles and is daily lived by thousands of sons and daughters of the Church. (2)

Can. 674. Totally contemplative institutes have a distinguished place in the Church: they praise God, they lead holy lives, they are of unseen help in the apostolate. They should never be called upon for apostolic work.

Supplementary Documentation

Decree on Religious Life: There are institutes which are entirely ordered towards contemplation, in such wise that their members give themselves over to God alone in solitude and silence, in constant prayer and willing penance. These will always have an honored place in the mystical Body of Christ, in which "all the members do not have the same function" (Rom 12:4), no matter how pressing may be the needs of the active ministry. For they offer to God an exceptional sacrifice of praise, they lend luster to God's people with abundant fruits of holiness, they sway them by their example, and they enlarge the Church by their hidden apostolic fruitfulness. They are thus an ornament to the Church and a fount of heavenly graces.

Decree on Bishops: Especially in view of the urgent needs of souls and of the lack of diocesan clergy, those religious institutes which are not dedicated to a purely contemplative life may be called upon by the bishop to help in various pastoral ministries. The special character of each religious institute should be taken into consideration. Superiors should make every effort to cooperate, even taking responsibility for parishes on a temporary basis. (35)

Can. 675, 1, 2, 3. Apostolic activity is of the nature of apostolic institutes, their whole life should be imbued with an apostolic spirit and their apostolic activity with the religious spirit. It should flow from union with God and should be done at the Church's behest and in communion with it.

Supplementary Documentation

Decree on Religious Life: In the Church there are very many institutes, clerical and lay, engaged in different kinds of apostolic work and endowed with gifts which vary according to the grace that is given to them. Administrators are given the gift of administration, the teacher the gift of doctrine, the preacher persuasiveness. Liberality is given to those who give to others, and cheerfulness to those who perform works of mercy (cf. Rom 12:5-8). "There are varieties of gifts, but the same Spirit" (1 Cor 12:4).

In these institutes, apostolic and charitable activity is of the very nature of religious life, as their own holy ministry and work of charity, entrusted to them by the Church and to be performed in its name. For this reason, the entire religious life of the members should be imbued with an apostolic spirit, and all their apostolic activity with a religious spirit. In order, therefore, that the members may first answer their call to follow Christ and to serve Christ himself in his members, their apostolic activity must needs have its source in intimate union with him. It is thus that their very love for God and their neighbor is fostered. (8)

Const. on the Church: It is not only through the sacraments and the ministrations of the Church that the Holy Spirit makes holy the People, leads them and enriches them with his virtues. Allotting his gifts according as he wills (cf. Cor 12:11), he also distributes special graces among the faithful of every rank. By these gifts he makes them fit and ready to undertake various tasks and offices for the renewal and building up of the Church, as it is written, "the manifestation of the Spirit is given to everyone for profit" (1 Cor 12:7). Whether these charisms be very remarkable or more simple and widely diffused, they are to be received with thanksgiving and consolation since they are fitting and useful for the needs of the Church. Extraordinary gifts are not to be rashly desired, nor is it from them that the fruits of apostolic labors are to be presumptuously expected. (12)

Can. 676. Lay institutes share in the Church's mission by works of spiritual and corporal mercy and should remain faithful to their vocation.

Supplementary Documentation

Decree on Religious Life: Lay religious life, for men and for women, is a state for the profession of the evangelical counsels which is complete in itself. The holy synod holds it in high esteem, for it is so useful to the Church in the exercise of its pastoral duty of educating the young, caring for the sick, and in its other ministries. It confirms the members in their vocation and urges them to adapt their life to modern requirements. (10)

Can. 677. Religious should retain their institute's apostolic work, but should adapt it to changing times.

2. They should impart their family spirit to any lay associations connected with them.

Supplementary Documentation

Decree on Religious Life: Institutes should faithfully maintain and accomplish the tasks that are theirs. Further mindful of what is useful for the universal Church and for the dioceses, they should adapt their ministry to the needs of time and place. They should employ appropriate and even new means, rejecting those which nowadays are less suited to the spirit and native genius of their institute.

The missionary spirit must, absolutely, be preserved in religious institutes and must be adapted to modern conditions, in keeping with the character of each, so that the preaching of the Gospel to all nations may be more effective. (20)

Can. 678, 1. Religious are subject to bishops with regard to public worship and the apostolate.

2. Religious remain subject to their own superiors while engaged in an external apostolate and bishops should remind them of this.

3. Bishops and superiors should collaborate in these matters.

Supplementary Documentation

Decree on Bishops: Religious should at all times treat the bishops, as the successors of the apostles, with loyal respect and reverence. Moreover, whenever legitimately called upon to do apostolic work, they must carry out these duties in such a way as to be the auxiliaries of the bishop and subject to him. Furthermore, religious should comply promptly and faithfully with the requests or desires of the bishops when they are asked to undertake a greater share in the ministry of salvation. Due consideration should be given to the character of the particular institute and to its constitutions, which may, if necessary, be adapted for this purpose in accord with the principles of this decree of the Council. (1)

Religious who are engaged in the external apostolate should be inspired by the spirit of their own institute, should remain faithful to the observance of their rule, and should be obedient to their superiors. Bishops should not fail for their part to insist on this obligation. (2)

All religious, whether exempt or non-exempt, are subject to the authority of the local ordinary in the following matters: public worship, without prejudice, however, to the diversity of rites; the care of souls; preaching to the people; the religious and moral education, catechetical instruction and liturgical formation of the faithful, especially of children. They are also subject to diocesan rules regarding the comportment proper to the clerical state and also the various activities relating to the exercise of their sacred apostolate. Catholic schools conducted by religious are also subject to the local ordinaries as regards their general policy and supervision without prejudice, however, to the right of the religious to manage them. Likewise, religious are obliged to observe all those prescriptions which episcopal councils or conferences legitimately decree as binding on all. (4)

Organized cooperation should be encouraged between the various religious institutes and between them and the diocesan clergy. There should be the closest possible coordination of all apostolic works and activities. This will depend mainly on a supernatural attitude of heart and mind grounded on charity. It is the responsibility of the Apostolic See to foster this coordination in regard to the universal Church; it is for each bishop to do so in his own diocese, and for the patriarchs and episcopal synods and conferences in their territories.

There should be consultations beforehand between bishops or episcopal conferences and religious superiors or conferences of major superiors, with regard to apostolic activities to be undertaken by religious. (5)

In order to promote harmonious and fruitful relations between the bishops and religious, the bishops and superiors should meet at regular intervals and as often as seems opportune to discuss business matters of general concern to their territory. (6)

Norms on Bishops: Even if a recognized exemption of religious, within the limits of law, should exist in mission territories, yet because of the special circumstances affecting the exercise of the sacred ministry in these places, in accordance with the Decree *Ad gentes divinitus*, the special statutes given or approved by the Apostolic See should be observed regarding relations between the local ordinary and the religious superior, particularly in the matter of a mission entrusted to a particular institute. (24)

Whenever a work of the apostolate is entrusted to any religious institute by a local ordinary in accordance with the prescriptions of law, a written agreement shall be made between the local ordinary and the competent superior of the institute which will, amongst other things, set down precisely all that concerns the work to be done, the members of the institute assigned to it and the finances.

For works of this nature members of the religious institute who are really suitable should be selected by the religious superior after discussion with the local ordinary and, where an ecclesiastical office is to be conferred on a member of the institute, the religious should be nominated by the local ordinary himself for a definite time decided upon by mutual agreement, his own superior presenting the candidate or at least assenting to the nomination. (30)

Even when a task is assigned to a religious by the local ordinary or by the episcopal conference, it shall be done with the consent of his superior and by means of a written agreement. (31)

In accordance with number 35 of the Decree *Christus Dominus* the general regulation of the Catholic schools of religious institutes, without prejudice to their rights in the government of these schools and while observing the norms laid down there [no. 35, (5)] concerning previous consultation between bishops and religious superiors, involve the general distribution of all the Catholic schools of the diocese, their cooperation with one another and their supervision, so that they shall be no less adapted than other schools to cultural and social objectives.

The local ordinary may visit, in person or by a deputy, in accordance with the sacred Canons, all

schools of religious institutes, their colleges, oratories, recreational centers, clubs, hospitals, orphanages or other institutes of this nature engaged upon
works of religion or of charity whether of a spiritual
or temporal kind. (39)

Mutual Relations: First of all, the very nature of
apostolic action requires that Bishops give prece-
dence to interior recollection and to the life of
prayer. It requires also that religious, in conformity
with their distinctive nature, renew themselves in
depth and remain assiduous in prayer.

Special care should be taken to promote 'the various undertakings aimed at establishing the contemplative life' since it holds a very honoured place in
the mission of the Church, 'no matter how pressing
may be the needs of the active ministry.' Especially
today, as the danger of materialism is growing more
serious, the vocation of all to the perfection of love is
illustrated with radical evidence by Institutes
entirely dedicated to contemplation, in which it is
more clearly manifest that, as St. Bernard says, 'the
motive for loving God is God and the measure of
love is love without measure'.

The activity of the People of God in the world is
by its nature universal and missionary, because of
the very character of the Church and the mandate of
Christ which confers on the apostolate a universality without limitations. Bishops and Superiors must
pay attention to this apostolic dimension and take
concrete initiatives to promote it.

The particular Church is the frame of history in
which a vocation expresses itself in concrete form
and fulfils its apostolic responsibility. It is here,
within the ambit of a definite culture, that the Gospel is preached and received. It is necessary, therefore, that this fact, which is of such importance for
pastoral renewal, should be kept in mind during the
work of formation.

The mutual influences between the two poles, namely between active participation within a particular culture and the perspective of universality, must be founded on an unalterable esteem and constant maintenance of those values of unity which must in no way be abandoned, the unity of the Catholic Church — for all the faithful — and that of the religious Institute — for all its members. Any local community breaking away from this unity would be exposed to a twofold danger: 'on the one hand, the danger of segregation, which produces sterility; on the other, the danger of losing one's own liberty when separated from the head; isolated, it becomes subject in many ways to the forces of those who attempt to subdue and exploit it.'

Men of our times very much expect from Religious that charismatic authenticity — alive and ingenious in its initiatives — which was most eminent in their Founders — so that they may more diligently and zealously engage in the apostolic work of the Church among those who today constitute the greater part of human kind, and are specifically beloved of the Lord: the *little ones* and the *poor* (Mt 18:1-6; Lk 6, 20). (23)

Associations of men and women religious, at diocesan level, have proved very useful. They should, therefore, be encouraged — with due consideration for their distinctive character and specific purpose:

(a) both as means of mutual liaison, of promotion and renewal of religious life in fidelity to the Magisterium and to the distinctive character of each Institute,

(b) and as a means for the discussion of 'mixed problems' between Bishops and Religious and for the co-ordination of the activities of religious families with the pastoral action of the diocese under the guidance of the Bishop. This, without prejudice to the relations and negotiations which can be carried

on directly by the Bishop himself with any individual Institute. (59)
(See also *Mutual Relations*, nos. 22, 54, 63, 64, 66)

Can. 679. A bishop, for a most serious reason, may forbid a religious to stay in his diocese if the superior has failed to act.

Can. 680. Co-operation is encouraged between institutes themselves and with the diocesan clergy, as is co-ordination of activity.

Supplementary Documentation

Decree on Bishops: Organized cooperation should be encouraged between the various religious institutes and between them and the diocesan clergy. There should be the closest possible coordination of all apostolic works and activities. This will depend mainly on a supernatural attitude of heart and mind grounded on charity. It is the responsibility of the Apostolic See to foster this coordination in regard to the universal Church; it is for each bishop to do so in his own diocese, and for the patriarchs and episcopal synods and conferences in their territories.

There should be consultations beforehand between bishops or episcopal conferences and religious superiors or conferences of major superiors, with regard to apostolic activities to be undertaken by religious.

In order to promote harmonious and fruitful relations between the bishops and religious, the bishops and superiors should meet at regular intervals and as often as seems opportune to discuss matters of general concern in their territory. (35)

Can. 681, 1. Work undertaken by religious at the request of a bishop is under his control, but see Can. 678, 2 and 3.

2. A written agreement should be drawn up to cover the matter (see under Can. 682).

Can. 682, 1. A bishop may appoint a religious to ecclesiastical office, with the superior's agreement.

2. The religious may be removed from office by bishop or superior.

Supplementary Documentation

Norms on Bishops: Whenever a work of the apostolate is entrusted to any religious institute by a local ordinary in accordance with the prescriptions of law, a written agreement shall be made between the local ordinary and the competent superior of the institute which will, amongst other things, set down precisely all that concerns the work to be done, the members of the institute assigned to it and the finances.

For works of this nature members of the religious institute who are really suitable should be selected by the religious superior after discussion with the local ordinary and, where an ecclesiastical office is to be conferred on a member of the institute, the religious should be nominated by the local ordinary himself for a definite time decided upon by mutual agreement, his own superior presenting the candidate or at least assenting to the nomination. (30)

Even when a task is assigned to a religious by the local ordinary or by the episcopal conference, it shall be done with the consent of his superior and by means of a written agreement. (31)

Any religious member of an institute may for a grave cause be removed from an office entrusted to him either at the wish of the authority who entrusted him with the office, who should inform the religious superior, or by the superior, who should inform the authority who entrusted the office; this by equal right, the consent of the other party being required in neither case. Neither party is required to reveal to the other reasons for his action, much less to justify them. There remains the right to appeal *in devolutivo* to the Apostolic See. (32)

Can. 683, 1. A bishop has the right to visitate churches and oratories of religious frequented by the faithful, also schools and other institutions committed to religious, but not their houses of formation.

2. He can sort out abuses if the superior does not act. (See under Cans. 586, 1; 611).

Supplementary Documentation

Norms on Bishops: The episcopal conference in each country, having heard the views of religious superiors with an interest in the matter, may lay down rules concerning soliciting financial help. These rules are to be obeyed by all religious orders, including those who in their title of foundation are called and are in fact mendicant, without prejudice however to their right to quest.

Religious shall not proceed to invite financial assistance by public subscription without the consent of the local ordinaries where the subscriptions are collected. (27)

Religious shall promote with zeal the proper or particular works of each institute, that is those which with the approval of the Apostolic See are theirs from their foundation or have behind them a venerable tradition and have been recognized and prescribed in the institutions and particular laws of the institute. Religious shall pay special attention to the spiritual needs of the dioceses and foster brotherly relations with the diocesan clergy and with other institutes engaged upon work similar to their own. (28)

The local ordinary may visit, in person or by a deputy, in accordance with the sacred Canons, all schools of religious institutes, their colleges, oratories, recreational centers, clubs, hospitals, orphanages or other institutions of this nature engaged upon works of religion or of charity whether of a spiritual or temporal kind.

CHAPTER 6: SEPARATION OF MEMBERS FROM INSTITUTES

ARTICLE 1: TRANSFER FROM ONE INSTITUTE TO ANOTHER

Can. 684, 1. A member in perpetual vows can transfer to another religious institute with the consent of both supreme moderators and their councils.

Canonical Commentary

The permission of the Holy See is no longer required for transfer from one institute of religious life to another institute of religious life.

684, 2. After at least three years probation the religious makes perpetual profession in the new institute, or returns to the former institute, unless secularised.

3. A monk may transfer to another monastery of the same institute, federation or confederation with the permission of both major superiors and the chapter of the recipient monastery, without repeating profession.

4. An institute's law must determine the type and duration of probation.

5. The permission of the Holy See is required for transfer to or from a society of common life or a secular institute.

Canonical Commentary

In contrast to number 1, above, this is a matter of transfer from one *kind* of institute of consecrated life to another. The text makes no mention of the two other kinds of institutes of consecrated life, the order of virgins and the eremitic life.

Can. 685, 1. The previous rights and obligations of a transferred religious are suspended pending profession, after which they cease.

ARTICLE 2: DEPARTURE FROM AN INSTITUTE

Can. 686, 1. The supreme moderator and council may permit exclaustration of a perpetually professed religious for up to three years, beyond this it is a matter for the Holy See or the diocesan bishop.

2. The Holy See may permit exclaustration of nuns.

3. At the request of the appropriate superior the Holy See may impose exclaustration, but with fairness and charity.

Canonical Commentary

This form of exclaustration is imposed in cases where the peace of a community has been seriously disturbed, but there are not sufficient grounds for dismissal. Imposed exclaustration is not prescribed for any definite period of time, but of itself it is not perpetual. It lasts as long as the reasons for it remain, but the person can be taken back only with the permission of the Sacred Congregation for Religious and Secular Institutes.

Can. 687. Exclaustrated persons are released from the obligations which are incompatible with their state, are under the care of their superior, may be permitted to wear the habit, but have no vote.

Canonical Commentary

This legislation differs considerably from that in the previous code (Can. 639).

Can. 688, 1. At the end of temporary profession, a person may leave.

2. The supreme moderator and council may dispense temporary vows in institutes of pontifical law. The bishop's confirmation is needed in other cases.

Can. 689, 1. The major superior may refuse subsequent profession at the end of the period of temporary profession.

2. Sufficient cause for this refusal is provided by physical or psychological illness incapacitating the person for the life of the institute, unless the illness is due to work done for the institute or to the institute's negligence.

3. Professed religious who become insane may not be expelled.

Can. 690, 1, 2. The supreme moderator or the superior of a monastery *'sui juris,'* with their councils, may re-admit a person who had left after novitiate or after profession, without requiring repetition of the novitiate, but after a period of probation.

Supplementary Documentation

Instruction on Renewal: When a member has left his Institute legitimately, either at the expiration of his temporary profession or commitment or after dispensation from these obligations, and later requests re-admission, the superior general, with the consent of his council, may grant this re-admission without the obligation of prescribing the repetition of the notiviate.

The superior general must, none the less, impose on him/her a certain period of probation, upon the completion of which the candidate may be admitted to temporary vows or commitment for a period of no less than one year, or no less than the period of temporary probation which he would have had to complete before profession at the time he left the institute. The superior may also demand a longer period of trial. (38)

Can. 691, 1, 2. A finally professed member who wants to leave — and it should be only for the most serious reasons — should present his/her petition to the supreme moderator who will present it to the Holy See if it is an institute of pontifical law, to the bishop if it is an institute of diocesan law.

Can. 692. Acceptance of an indult to leave automatically dispenses a person from vows and from all obligations contracted at profession.

Can. 693. If it is a cleric who is leaving, the indult is not granted until he is accepted into a diocese, at least on an experimental basis.

ARTICLE 3: THE DISMISSAL OF MEMBERS.

Can. 694, 1. Dismissal from an institute follows automatically on (1) public defection from the Catholic faith (2) marriage or attempted, even civil, marriage.

2. In such cases, the major superior and council should establish the facts and state what has happened, so that the dismissal will be juridically established.

Can. 695, 1. A member must be dismissed if guilty of the following transgressions: murder, or detention, mutilation or grave bodily harm (Can. 1397); procuring an abortion (Can. 1398); living in concubinage or remaining in a situation of external sin against the sixth commandment (Can. 1395, 1). The superior may decide on some other way of dealing with a person guilty of a sexual offence involving force or threats or a minor or in public (Can. 1395, 2).

2. The accused must be apprised of the accusation and of the proof by the major superior and must be given the opportunity of self-defence. The documentation, signed by the major superior, the accused and a notary, must be sent to the supreme moderator.

Can. 696, 1. Dismissal can also be incurred because of other grave, external, imputable and provable violations of the vows, scandalous behaviour, unrepentant diffusion of condemned doctrines, public espousal of atheistic or materialistic ideology, unlawful absence. An institute may add to the list.

2. Less serious offences, as determined by the institute, suffice for dismissal from temporary vows.

Can. 697. The following procedure is to be followed by the major superior if it is decided to go ahead with the process of dismissal: (1) the proof is assembled, (2) the member is warned about what will happen and is given an opportunity of self-defence and the warning is repeated in a fortnight if necessary, (3) if this in turn fails the process of dismissal is initiated.

Can. 698. In the foregoing cases, the accused member may deal directly with the supreme moderator.

Can. 699, 1. The supreme moderator with his council considers the charge and if satisfied issues the dismissal, giving the reasons.

2. In monasteries described in Can. 615, the matter is referred to the bishop.

Can. 700. A decree of dismissal is not effective until confirmed by the Holy See or, for institutes of diocesan law, the bishop and it must indicate that there is a right of appeal within ten days.

Can. 701. Legitimate dismissal negates vows, rights and obligations arising from profession. A dismissed cleric may not exercise holy orders unless he finds a bishop willing to accept him or at least allow him to exercise his orders.

Can. 702, 1, 2. Persons who legitimately leave or are expelled from an institute have no claim on it for work done on its behalf, but the institute should treat such a person fairly and with charity.

Can. 703. If there is grave external scandal or danger of most serious damage to the institute, a person may be ejected forthwith from a religious house by the major superior or, if the danger is imminent, the local superior and council. The major superior may institute a process or refer the matter to the Holy See.

Can. 704. The Holy See should be informed about those who leave or are dismissed (see Can. 592, 1).

CHAPTER 7: RELIGIOUS RAISED TO THE EPISCOPACY

Can. 705. A religious who becomes a bishop remains a member of his institute but owes obedience to the pope alone.

Can. 706, 1, 2, 3. The duties and rights of a bishop-religious depend on the extent of the renunciation of property made by him at profession (Can. 668), the nature of the property and the intention of the person making a donation.

Can. 707, 1, 2. A retired bishop-religious may normally live where he wants and his material needs will be met either by arrangement of the conference of bishops (Can. 402, 2), by his own institute if it wishes, or by the Holy See.

CHAPTER 8: CONFERENCES OF MAJOR SUPERIORS

Can. 708. Conferences of major superiors can help by assisting individual institutes to fulfil their mission, by conducting business of common concern, or inaugurating cooperation with the conference of bishops or with individual bishops.

Supplementary Documentation

Decree on Religious Life: Conferences or councils of major superiors, erected by the Holy See, are to be welcomed. They can contribute a great deal towards the fuller achievement of the purpose of the individual institutes, towards fostering more effective cooperation for the good of the Church, towards a more equitable distribution of ministers of the Gospel in a given territory, and towards treating the problems which are common to all religious.

They should establish suitable coordination and cooperation with episcopal conferences with regard to the exercise of the apostolate.

Conferences of this type can also be established for secular institutes. (23)

Mutual Relations: Within the setting of religious life, the Holy See establishes Conferences of major superiors and unions of superiors general, at the local and universal level. These, of course, differ from episcopal conferences in nature and authority. Their primary purpose is the promotion of religious life as it is inserted in the structures of the mission of the Church. Their activity consists in offering common services such as fraternal initiatives and proposals for collaboration, always with due respect to the distinctive character of each Institute. This also contributes to giving effective assistance for pastoral co-ordination, especially if at fixed times proper revision is made of the working statutes, and above all, 'in conformity with the directives of the Holy See, mutual relations are maintained between the conferences of bishops and the conferences of major superiors.' (21)

Can. 709. Conferences of major superiors can be established as 'juridical persons' by the Holy See, to which they are subject and which approves their statutes.

Canonical Commentary

The conferences are not subject to the episcopal conference or the local bishop, except in those matters in which religious are subject to bishops — see under Can. 678.

Title III: Secular Institutes

Can. 710. In secular institutes the faithful, living in the world, try to achieve perfect charity and to contribute to the world's salvation from inside it.

Canonical Commentary

Secular institutes received official approval as a special vocation in the Church in the Constitution *Provida Mater Ecclesia*, by Pope Pius XII, in 1947. They are not religious. While consecrated to God through baptism and the profession of the evangelical counsels, they live a secular life. Their apostolate is essentially one of presence in the world. Their way of life is different from the conventual life of religious, but it is not distinguished from the way of life of the rest of the faithful by 'flight from the world: *fuga mundi*' which is sociologically affirmed in the demands of community life. They are distinguished from the rest of the laity in that they are consecrated persons by reason of their profession of the evangelical counsels.

Can. 711. Members of secular institutes are either clerics or lay people.

Can. 712. Their constitutions must define the kind of promises by which they profess the evangelical counsels and the obligations they take on.

Canonical Commentary

The promises which they make are not public.

Can. 713, 1, 2, 3. Members of secular institutes endeavour to insert the gospel spirit through the world. Their lay members exercise an apostolate in the world and by means of the world, by the witness of their lives, by ordering temporal affairs in God's way and by their service to the ecclesial community. Their clerical members offer the witness of a consecrated life, help their fellow priests and exercise their priestly ministry.

Supplementary Documentation

Decree on Religious Life: While it is true that secular institutes are not religious institutes, at the same time they involve a true and full profession of the evangelical counsels in the world, recognized by the Church. This profession confers a consecration on people living in the world, men and women, laymen and clerics. Therefore they should make it their chief aim to give themselves to God totally in perfect charity. The institutes themselves ought to preserve their own special character — their secular character, that is to say — to the end that they may be able to carry on effectively and everywhere the apostolate in the world and, as it were, from the world, for which they were founded.

Let them know quite clearly, at the same time, that they will be unable to accomplish so great a task unless the members have so thorough a grounding in matters divine and human that they will be truly leaven in the world, for the strengthening and increase of the Body of Christ. Superiors therefore should devote great care to the formation, especially the spiritual formation, of their subjects, and also to the promotion of their higher studies. (11)

Can. 714. Members live ordinary lives, alone, with their families, or together.

Canonical Commentary

Living together can provide mutual support. But it also involves the possibility of approximating closer to conventual consecrated life. An over-emphasis on living together could be detrimental to the identity of the secular institute.

Can. 715, 1. Clerical members incardinated in a diocese come under the bishop, save for the consecrated life.

2. If incardinated in their own institute (Can. 266, 3) they relate to the bishop much as do religious priests.

Can. 716, 1, 2. Members should share in their institute's life, fostering a spirit of unity.

Can. 717, 1, 2, 3. An institute's constitutions must determine the mode of government, of selection of moderators and their term of office. Only full members can be moderators and it is their task to foster unity and involvement.

Can. 718. Administration of property is governed by book five of the code of Canon law and by their own laws, which must define the institute's economic obligations to members.

Can. 719, 1, 2, 3, 4. Since the success of the members' apostolate and their fidelity to their vocation depends on their union with Christ, the following are prescribed: prayer, reading of the scriptures, annual retreat and other spiritual exercises, daily Mass, frequent confession, spiritual direction, perhaps from their moderators.

Can. 720. The right of admission to institutes belongs to major superiors and their councils.

Can. 721, 1. The following cannot be validly admitted: a person under eighteen, a professed member of a religious order or a member of a society of apostolic life, a married person.
  2. The constitutions may add to this list, or impose conditions.
  3. A candidate must be mature.

Canonical Commentary

The 'conditions' mentioned in number 2 are considered to refer to liceity — that is, they would make admission illegal, but not invalid.

Can. 722, 1, 2, 3. The constitutions should define the form and duration of the period of probation, which must last for at least two years and in which candidates will have the opportunity of discerning their own and their institute's vocation, will learn its way of life and how to channel an evangelical way of life into the institute's apostolate.

Can. 723, 1, 2, 3, 4. After the period of probation those who persevere will be admitted to a first temporary 'incorporation' for at least five years, after which those judged suitable will be admitted to final 'incorporation' by permanently-renewable 'bonds.'

Can. 724, 1, 2. The members' formation in matters divine and human is to be continued after the period of probation and the moderator should see to their spiritual formation.

Can. 725. An institute may bring into association with itself other members of the faithful who wish to live by its spirit and share in its mission.

Can. 726, 1. At the end of temporary incorporation, a person may leave or be asked to leave by the supreme moderator and his council.

2. During temporary incorporation a member may be granted permission to leave by the supreme moderator, for a grave cause.

Can. 727, 1. A permanently incorporated member may, at the request of the supreme moderator be granted permission to leave by the Holy See, if the institute is of pontifical right, by the diocesan bishop if it is of diocesan right.

2. For a cleric incardinated in the institute, see Can. 693.

Can. 728. All links, rights and obligations contracted cease with the granting of an indult to leave.

Can. 729. Dismissal of members is to be done in accordance with Cans. 694, 695, 697-700 and 701.

Can. 730 Transfer from one secular institute to another is done as prescribed in Cans. 684, 1, 2, 4 and 685. For transfer to or from another institute of consecrated life, permission of the Holy See is required.

SECTION II: SOCIETIES OF APOSTOLIC LIFE

Can. 731, 1. Members of societies of apostolic life do not take vows, they endeavour to achieve the apostolic purpose of their society, live in common and make the perfection of charity their aim.

2. Members of some of these societies commit themselves to the observance of the evangelical counsels by some bond.

Canonical Commentary

The historical origins of these societies of apostolic life can be traced to the sixteenth century. At that time there were many communities of women who imitated the life of nuns, wore a religious habit, but did not take solemn vows, which were required of religious, and did not observe cloister. Saint Pius V had insisted on cloister for nuns and as a result Saint Francis de Sales imposed solemn vows and cloister on the Sisters of the Visitation, an institute founded to visit the poor and the sick. But St. Vincent de Paul obtained approval for the Daughters of Charity, who were also dedicated to visiting the sick. But in order to obtain approval they avoided too close a resemblance to religious; they wore lay dress, were considered laywomen in the eyes of Church law and when they pronounced their vows they did so without ceremony. Pius V had also ordered certain institutes of men who were living a common life and wearing a habit distinct from the dress of the diocesan clergy to pronounce solemn vows or to leave their communities. However, to meet the needs of the Church, many new foundations of priests living in common were made. They did not take public vows and dressed like the diocesan clergy.

Can. 732. Canons 578-597 apply to societies of apostolic life. Canons 598-602 also apply to the societies mentioned in 731, 1.

Can. 733, 1. The society itself is empowered to establish a house and local community, with the written consent of the bishop, who must also be consulted if it is to be suppressed.

2. Such consent carried entitlement to at least an oratory in which the eucharist is celebrated and reserved.

Can. 734. A society's constitutions should determine its mode of government.

Can. 735, 1, 2, 3. A society's laws must define how members are admitted — subject to the provisions of Cans. 642-645 — their probation, incorporation and formation.

Can. 736, 1, 2. In clerical societies, clerics are incardinated in the society, normally, but in their studies and reception of orders they follow the regulations for diocesan priests.

Can. 737. Members derive rights and obligations from their incorporation, which gives them into the care of the society.

Can. 738, 1, 2, 3. Members are subject to their moderators in their internal lives and discipline, to the diocesan bishop with regard to public worship and the apostolate, having regard to Cans. 679-683. Relations between a priest incardinated in a diocese and the bishop are a separate matter.

Can. 739. Apart from the obligations imposed by their societies, members are subject to the obligations common to all clerics.

Can. 740. Members must live in a house or community, observing the common life according to the rule of the institute.

Can. 741, 1. The societies, their parts and their houses can acquire, possess, administer and alienate property in accordance with book five of the code of Canon law and with Cans. 636, 638 and 639.

2. Their members, also, can acquire, possess, administer and dispose of property.

Can. 742. A society's own constitutions make provision for the departure or dismissal of the temporarily incorporated.

Can. 743. The supreme moderator may grant permission to leave to a finally-incorporated member, with the consent of the council, but for a clerical member, see Can. 693.

Can. 744, 1, 2. The supreme moderator and council may grant permission for a transfer of a finally-incorporated member to another society of apostolic life, but only the Holy See can grant transfer to or from an institute of consecrated life.

Can. 745. The supreme moderator and his council can permit a finally-incorporated member to live outside the society for up to three years, without the rights and obligations incompatible with that state, but under the moderator's care. If the member is a cleric, the permission of the bishop is needed.

Can. 746. The dismissal of a finally-incorporated member is to be governed by Cans. 694-704.

Concluding Canonical Commentary

The new code has made a serious attempt to be faithful to the mind of the Council in drafting the new legislation. But the very fact that the 1977 draft had to be abandoned is indicative of the problems that the subcommission faced in trying to be faithful to the mind of the Council. Many superiors requested more detailed legislation. Nevertheless, the Code applies the principle of subsidiarity in many places. Each institute has the responsibility of being faithful to its own charism. Thus it is left to the various institutes to draw up their own specific legislation in many matters.

Down through the centuries there have been many different forms of living the evangelical counsels. There has been considerable discussion about how to define the essential elements of the consecrated life. The law which has been presented to the Church is an attempt to express in juridical language what is a charismatic way of life. The Spirit will continue to inspire new ways of living the evangelical counsels.

APPENDIX

APPENDIX

Digest of other Canons and portions of Canons referred to in the preceding text as applying to institutes of consecrated life.

Elections and Other Decisions

Can. 119. Unless the law says otherwise, an absolute majority is required in elections, a majority of the potential voters being present. If a third ballot is needed, the choice must lie between the two with the most votes, or between the two oldest of those with most votes. If there is a tie, the oldest is deemed elected. For other business, an absolute majority is required, the chairperson deciding if there is a tie after two ballots. Unanimous approval needed for whatever affects everybody individually.

Power of Government

Can. 131, 1. Ordinary power of government goes with office, delegation is given to a person.

2. Ordinary power can be exercised by office holders or vicars.

3. Person claiming delegation must be able to prove it.

Can. 133. To exceed the limits of delegation is to nullify it, but not normally if one merely departs from the method determined.

Can. 137, 1, 2, 3, 4. Ordinary executive power may normally be delegated; power delegated by the Holy See and, to a lesser extent, power delegated by another authority having ordinary power may be subdelegated. Subdelegated power may not normally be again subdelegated.

Can. 138. Ordinary executive power and power delegated for all cases are to be widely interpreted, not other forms of delegated power. Delegation is understood to carry what is needed to do the job.

Can. 139, 1, 2. Normally, the executive power of one authority is not suspended by an appeal to another authority, but normally a lesser authority must not interfere when a matter is referred to a higher authority.

Can. 140, 1, 2, 3. When a number have been delegated to a task *en bloc*, (the normal presumption) the first person to start is normally deemed entrusted with sole responsibility. If delegated to function collegially, they must proceed as in Can. 119.

Can. 141. If several have been delegated successively, the first of them should do the job.

Can. 142, 1. Delegated power ceases with the mandate, or when the period or the number of cases or the purpose have gone or when withdrawn, not normally with the ending of the delegating power.

Can. 142, 2. Internal actions are valid if done inadvertently after time of delegation.

Can. 143, 1. A person loses ordinary power when he/she goes out of office.

2. Ordinary power is suspended pending an appeal against removal from office.

Can. 144. When a person acts 'in common error' or 'positive doubt' about law or fact, the Church makes up for it.

Glossary of Some
Technical Terms

GLOSSARY OF SOME TECHNICAL TERMS

aggregation: A process by which an institute joins another institute with itself in an association which is spiritual, involving no juridical dependence and no sacrifice of the other institute's autonomy.

alienation of property: Transfer of ownership or of use of property to the detriment of the 'stable patrimony' (q.v.) of an institute.

consecrated life, institutes of: A term covering religious orders and congregations, and secular institutes.

consent (of council): A binding decision of council.

constitution: Collection of the more important, more stable legislation, approved by the Holy See. May not be changed save with permission of Holy See.

consultative vote (of council): Non-binding decision of council.

delegated power: Power granted to individuals by the law or by a person.

diocesan institute: An institute approved by a diocesan bishop, not confirmed by the Holy See.

directory: Collection of less important legislation, subject to change by the institute (This collection can have other names, too.).

exclaustration: Voluntary or imposed absence from an institute, while remaining under the care of the major superior.

extraordinary administration: Activities for which superiors and officials need special permission.

impediment to validity: Factor rendering an activity (of religious profession) invalid.

incorporation: The process by which a person becomes a member of an institute.

juridical person: An institute or part of an institute, or a community entitled to own and administer property.

monastery sui juris: An independent monastery.

ordinary administration: Activities which superiors and officials can perform on their own authority.

ordinary power: Power attached by the law to an office.

pontifical institute: An institute approved by the Holy See.

province: A section of an institute, with at least three houses, under a major superior.

public vow: A vow received in the name of the Church by the legitimate superior.

religious institute: An order or congregation with common life and public vows.

secular institute: Institute of consecrated life (q.v.) whose members profess the evangelical counsels and live in the world.

society of common life: An institute whose members live in common, do not take vows, but some make a promise to observe the evangelical counsels.

stable patrimony: What constitutes the basis of an institute's financial security.

INDEX

INDEX

N.B. All references are Canons and refer also to Supplementary Documentation and Canonical Commentary following them.

159

A SPECIAL KIND OF MARRYING

Prepared by a committee of priests involved
in Marriage and Family Life work in the
Archdiocese of Chicago, and tested in over
300 parishes.

**A SPECIAL
KIND OF
MARRYING**

Library of Congress
Catalogue No. 80-67686

ISBN No. 0-915388-09-X

Printed in the United States

Buckley Publications, Inc.
233 E. Erie St.   •   Chicago, Illinois 60611

Contents

Edited by: The Beacon Group
Cover art: Robert Fairman
Layout and Design: Marylou Draper

We wish to express our gratitude to Rev. Thomas Hickey, Rev. Ronald Kalas, Rev. Wm. McNulty, Rev. Joseph Mul-crone, Rev. George Rassas, and Mrs. Elizabeth Bannon for their special contribution to this publication.

Introduction

Interest in marriage preparation has been renewed throughout the country. Policies and guidelines have been developed in an effort to make premarital preparation a worthwhile experience both for the couple and for the priest who is responsible for that preparation. Through the use of these policies and guidelines, the priest's premarital ministry should be clarified, and the couple's relationship should be strengthened. However, although these policies and guidelines can aid the priest in his ministry, much still depends on the individual priest's ability to relate to the couple and his ability to hear and care about the couple's new life together.

This manual is the result of many hours and careful thought spent in conjunction with priests in the Archdiocese of Chicago who are concerned about and committed to Marriage and Family Life. The material presented in this manual, although helpful to anyone involved in marriage preparation, is designed primarily for the parish priest who encounters the engaged couple and who needs practical, helpful guidance in providing pastoral assistance to them.

1

The
Need
for
Policies

Good marriage preparation is based on three commonly accepted policies, which are enumerated below. *A Special Kind of Marrying* has been prepared to help clergy consider these policies in their ministry to engaged couples.

- More than ever before, the priest should be conscious of his responsibility for assessing a couple's readiness and potential for marriage while continuing to offer the couple all the help and support he can.

- At least four-to-six months should intervene between the couple's first visit to the rectory and the wedding date.

- Except in unusual circumstances, couples should be required to participate in a structured premarital preparation program.

These policies have their roots in several important premises. First, the Chruch has a unique and important message to communicate about the Christian vision of life, love, and fidelity, and about creativity, personal growth, and sacramentality. It can no longer be taken for granted that this message is communicated, as it was for centuries, in stable, homogeneous Catholic communities through which the message was handed down by formal education, tradition, custom, ritual, family values, and modelling. In a pluralistic society, replete with competing, confusing value systems, this message must be explicated and presented in a compelling way that makes sense.

Secondly, other factors that affect marriage—communication, sexuality, adjustment, roles—are important and must be given equal consideration.

Thirdly, our society is beset by a type of individualism and narcissism that encourages self-centeredness, applauds "doing your own thing," questions the possibility of commitment, trivializes sex, and denigrates children and the demands and constraints they place on a couple's freedom.

As an institution, marriage is in trouble. The divorce rate has been rising steadily for almost two decades, approximately 1,220,000 couples were divorced in 1979 alone.

Ministry to the engaged is important because the Church clearly has a stake in good marriages. The priest has the unique opportunity as counselor and religious educator to meet with adults in a positive context....courtship and engagement are a supremely important time in the life of a couple. If couples can be helped to use that time well, it can serve as a strong foundation for their entire married life. Furthermore, the engagement period is a "passage" time that presents the opportunity for new beginnings. During this period, many couples are especially open to personal growth and to renewed dedication to high ideals.

Ministry to the engaged is also important because the priest can make a reasonable assessment of a couple's readiness for marriage and can offer them help. If handled well, premarriage education programs can be very valuable and can enhance a couple's chances for a rewarding and satisfying life together.

Couples who clearly are not ready to enter a sacramental marriage should not be permitted to do so. Such couples should, however, be given every assistance and support they need before they are dismissed.

Invitation to Renaissance

The institution of premarriage guidelines is not to be interpreted as a "tightening up," an invitation to superscrutiny, or an encouragement to "up your quotas" and flunk more couples. It is to be interpreted as a challenge to priests, married couples, deacons, teachers, parishes—with whatever resources they can mobilize—and by agencies and marriage education programs to make a concerted effort to:

- learn more about marriage and the family in our society;
- take more time and develop more skills to discern the needs of young couples;
- offer them personal help and the support of the church community;
- design better educational and involvement programs; and
- find more effective ways to communicate our faith vision and the Christian ideal of marriage.

In a word, to call for and work for a renaissance in love, marriage, and the family—in a society that has become very confused about these important values.

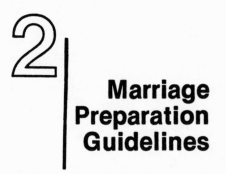

2 | Marriage Preparation Guidelines

Policies are clear, authoritative guidelines that direct decision making, specify procedures, and control activities under most circumstances. They should be the fruit of shared experience, based on significant values and objectives, mutually agreed upon, and adhered to consistently, but not rigidly. Their purpose is simply to avoid confusion and to solve problems.

Establish Policies

The policies that have been or are being adopted in dioceses across the country are called "A Common Policy for Marriage Preparation" or "Marriage Preparation Guidelines." Copies of and information about such guidelines can be obtained from dioceses that have established active policies (such as the Archdiocese of Chicago and the dioceses of New Jersey and Wisconsin).

The existence of a common policy or guidelines for marriage preparation throughout a diocese is not a prerequisite to *A Special Kind of Marrying.* A parish or an individual priest can establish norms. However, the more widespread the development of marriage preparation policies, the more likely the acceptance of these policies by priests and engaged couples. (In this book, reference is made to policies on the parish level, although the norms described can be modified and applied on the diocesan level as well.)

Content

Content of guidelines must be determined by the individual parish, perhaps based on the general criterion of what the parish community can do to be of greatest service to engaged couples and their families. Some priests have suggested that a booklet containing detailed information about practical arrangements based on policies should be distributed to every engaged couple.

Promulgation

Several years ago, a national poll revealed that 19% of all Americans could not name the president of the United States and over 40% could not name their state senator—although over 80% were conversant with the latest TV situation comedy. Despite their publication in Catholic magazines, papers, and parish bulletins, premarriage policies and guidelines will not become household words either. However, such policy and guidelines need to be published and publicized broadly for several reasons:

- to avoid misinterpretation of the policy and/or guidelines as a form of ecclesiastical "clamping down";

- to promote awareness among engaged couples and their families so they can plan accordingly; and

- to avoid angry reactions to inconsistent application of requirements. For example, "My sister was married last year, and she came in only seven weeks before the wedding." "My brother and his wife were not required to attend a premarriage program." "You can't do this to us, we already contracted for the hall and the band on the 23rd."

The parish policy can be promulgated by using periodic announcements in parish bulletins; making announcements from the pulpit which are accompanied by explanatory sermons; and making the policy available to the couple at or immediately after their first contact with the rectory.

Statement on Sacramental Policy*

The statement on sacremental policy should be positive and nonthreatening. Suggested wording for key paragraphs in the statement follows:

"To assure that parishes (priests) offer the greatest possible help and support to engaged couples, the diocese (parish) has developed the following guidelines.

- Couples contemplating marriage are requested not to set a firm wedding date until after they have come to the rectory and discussed their plans with a priest.

- Couples are asked to visit the rectory at least four-to-six months before the wedding date to ensure appropriate time for paperwork, planning, and liturgy preparation and adequate time to discuss and reflect on their upcoming marriage in the midst of hectic preparation.

---

*If "Statement on Sacramental Policy" does not suit you as a title, perhaps titles like "Guidelines for the Reception of the Sacraments at St. Drusilla's," "A Special Kind of Marrying," or "The First Season of Love" might have more appeal.

- Unless unusual circumstances exist, all couples will be asked to attend one of several interesting and stimulating premarriage education programs provided by the parish, the diocese, or the campus ministry."

Priests and Parish Problems

On occasion, certain parishes might have a pastor or associate who are stumbling blocks to effective premarriage ministry. Their mode of operation may take various forms and might be quite familiar to you.

"Marrying Sam" will join any two people in wedlock, if they are of opposite sexes and can get a license. His attitude may stem from a sense of kindness run amuk, from a boundless hope in mankind's potential for growth, or from a mixture of indifference and laziness.

The "Defender of the Bond" refuses 74% of the couples who present themselves and has grave doubts about the rest. He is certain that most couples do not have the required insight into the meaning of sacramentality. He might be a person who finds deep personality flaws in everyone, or he just might like to exercise power.

Or, there is the priest who thinks that couples need not attend marriage preparation sessions, and his opposite who would like to require a 30-day closed retreat for each prospective partner (made separately, of course).

Another problem arises in populous parishes that have 60 to 100 or more marriages per year. Let's say St. Mary's is blessed with Father A, who has an attractive personality, celebrates the Liturgy with great reverence, and preaches like Chrysostom; Father B who is reserved, standoffish, and hard to know; and a pastor who will only "take a marriage" if it is a state occasion (translate—involves the offspring of a politician, doctor, or major donor). The result is that 93% of all couples request Father A.

How do you handle this problem? Is it more important that the couples get the priest they want, or that marriages are distributed? If you opt for the latter, what does Father A say..."Sorry, my allotment is all filled up; I'll have to ask you to switch to Father B."?

Without belaboring the point,
PARISHES NEED POLICIES ON
MARRIAGE AND MARRIAGE PREPARATION.

3 | Couples
Couples
Couples

Although behaviorists have been able to develop profiles of the typical executive, successful NFL quarterback, or successful careerwoman, to develop a profile of a typical engaged couple is almost impossible. Either partner will run the gamut of potential personality traits and combinations thereof.

He, she, or they might be naive, shy, docile, credulous, bright, attractive, enthusiastic, open, cooperative, well-educated, experienced, sophisticated, pseudo-sophiscated, hostile, argumentative, immature, sullen, surly, dull, etc. Not to mention young, old, religious, irreligious, already married, or pregnant. In sum, no one since Adam has seen the world with pristine eyes.

Each of the men and women who comes before you has a significant, personal history that has shaped personalities and formed attitudes about marriage, roles, children, love, sex, money, religion, and Church. Your challenge is to discover these attitudes, meet the couples at their own levels, and help them grow and develop in their relationships.

Although each couple is different and unique, common features exist and are worth mentioning and thinking about. Among them are the problem of anticipatory dissolubility, the dyad factor, anxiety about the marriage decision, and hectic schedules before the wedding, all of which are discussed briefly below.

Anticipatory Dissolubility. Despite the fact that most young couples today enter marriage hoping for, desiring, and even planning a permanent relationship, they differ greatly in their attitudes when compared to engaged couples of a generation or two ago. Because divorce is now seen as a fact of life and a real possibility with which to contend in the future, young couples view divorce as a regrettable occurrence but a distinct possibility. In our society, divorce is an acceptable and a viable option for couples from almost every background—a possibility to be given serious consideration in many sets of circumstances.

Because of this pervasive attitude and because of the mounting statistics on divorce, numerous deleterious effects have occurred.

- Commitment to the indissolubility of marriage has decreased substantially. Couples face their commitment to one another rather tentatively.

- The threshold of tolerance between couples is lowered sharply and motivation for self-adjustment in marriage is sapped. (Partners committed to the indissolubility of their marriages would most likely say, "I'd better stop doing XX and start doing XYZ if we are going to make this marriage work.").

- Hope for strong, lasting marriage is weakened. Couples conclude that reaching their tenth anniversary is highly unlikely and set themselves on a path that just might prove their doubts to be realistic. "If I can keep my marriage together while all those around me are breaking theirs, I must be strange."

The Dyad Factor. For the first time in their lives, engaged couples must start thinking in terms of "we." Their private worlds are breached in a special way. Trying to discern what the other needs, wants, and prefers, while maintaining their own individuality, can lead to compromise and negotiation that often causes stress.

Before Marriage Jitters. The decision to marry, once made, is still fringed with doubt for some couples. Should I have? Is he/she the one? Is now the time? Am I ready? Will I be able to handle it? Occasionally, periods of minor depression can occur in one or both partners. If the other partner picks up signs of hesitation, anxiety mounts, and discomfort or doubt snowballs.

Hectic Schedules. Over 25 areas must be handled and over 200 decisions must be made in planning a wedding— all in a relatively short period of time. For the first time in-laws must be considered. Schedules become tighter and hectic; nerves become frazzled and tempers short. As another potential source of stress and friction, marriage preparation must be handled carefully, with compassion and humor.

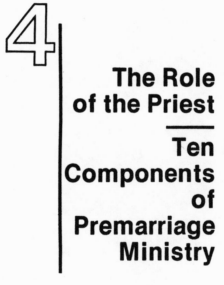

4

**The Role
of the Priest**

**Ten
Components
of
Premarriage
Ministry**

The parish priest who accepts the responsibility for pre-marriage ministry must be able to wear at least ten different hats. He must be a good host, a facilitator, an educator, a theologian, an evaluator, an official witness, a counselor, a consultant, a celebrant, a friend, and a confidant. In each of these roles, the priest is challenged to help the engaged couple prepare for their long life together and prepare in a fashion that brings them closer to the Christian vision of life and love. However, the priest must also be realistic in his expectations for his ministry with couples. (For a comparison of realistic and unrealistic expectations for premarriage ministry, see pages 32-33.) The priest fulfills these ten roles in the manner described below.

§

As a *good host*, he invites a couple into the marriage preparation process and orchestrates it for them according to their individual needs and circumstances.

As a *facilitator*, he helps a couple reflect on, discuss, and gain greater understanding of each other, their life situation, the basis for and the potential of their relationship, the challenges before them, and the meaning of marriage.

§

As an *educator*, the priest opens a couple to deeper insights regarding the complex dimensions of marriage in our modern society.

§

As a *theologian*, he awakens, stirs up and/or strives to deepen a couple's understanding of Church and their vision of the Christian commitment at the core of a sacramental marriage.

§

The priest as an *evaluator* assesses a couple's maturity, sincerity, the depth of their relationship, and their canonical, religious, psychological, and practical readiness for marriage.

§

He represents the teachings, traditions, and support of the Christian community as an *official witness*, and in this capacity may, on occasion, have to delay or refuse to perform a marriage.

§

As a *counselor*, the priest might have to provide special help to certain couples or refer them to sources where they can find special help. In these instances, the priest must be sensitive to the couple's needs and monitor their progress.

§

In his role as *consultant*, the priest helps with paperwork and with the practical details of the wedding and the wedding ceremony.

§

In his role as *celebrant*, he seeks to provide a rich liturgical experience for the couple and their families and friends— one that is memorable and truly celebrates and manifests the momentous step that the couple is taking.

§

And, finally, but perhaps most importantly, the priest as *confidant* and *friend* supports and counsels a couple at one of the most important times of their lives. Hopefully, he leaves the couple with positive feelings toward the role of the Church in their lives and toward the priest himself.

	QUESTIONABLE/UNREALISTIC
Couples	All couples are alike. All couples are anxious. All couples are secure.
Establishing Rapport	I will establish a close personal relationship with every couple and maintain contact with them after the wedding day.
Assessing Readiness	I can find out everything significant about this couple and understand their deepest feelings and thoughts. I can determine fully their readiness for marriage and be definitive about their chances of success.
Religious Dimension	I must, if necessary, supply a complete religious education program for them and totally change certain religious attitudes.
Preparing a Couple for Married Life	I must tell this couple exactly what marriage is about, for their future happiness depends on how much I do for them. The couple will understand and accept everything I have to tell them.
Preparing the Liturgy	Every couple shares the same feeling about the importance of liturgy and is able to plan, personalize, and prepare the liturgy themselves.

TABLE 1. Comparison of Unrealistic and Realistic Expectations in Premarriage Ministry.

	REALISTIC
Couples	Every couple is different. I must seek to discern their particular attitudes, expectations, and needs.
Establishing Rapport	By giving them time, interest, and respect, by sharing feelings and insights, I will let them know that I am concerned about them as people that I consider their marriage important, and that the Church cares about them.
Assessing Readiness	I can encourage them to trust and be open in dialogue. I can determine their reasonable, basic readiness to accept the responsibilities of marriage.
Religious Dimension	I can offer a meaningful vision of Christian marriage as an ideal; I can give them a positive experience of the Church; and I can explore their openness to faith and encourage fuller participation in the life of the Church.
Preparing a Couple for Married Life	Some things can be done only by themselves; I cannot radically change behavior. I *can* teach couples some realities, skills, and resources for their marriage; I can persuade most of them about the importance of marriage preparation; and I can assist them in the process of communication.
Preparing the Liturgy	With help, couples can develop a greater understanding of liturgy and, with time and explanations, they can personalize the liturgy and make it a prayer and a celebration.

5

The Priest's Objectives and Agenda

The following section itemizes the priest's objectives and agenda for each of three suggested sessions with the engaged couple. Although three sessions are strongly recommended, if only two sessions can be held with the couple, these should be the initial session and one follow-up session, held after the couple has attended a premarriage education program.

Session One: Initial Contact

- Establish rapport,

- Present and validate your position,

- Recognize the couple's agenda,

- Get to know the couple by engaging them in a dialogue on key questions regarding their background, attitudes, and expectations of marriage,

- Share insights and information,

- Explore the faith dimension,

- Deal with the question of interfaith marriage, if appropriate,

- Persuade them to attend a premarriage education program,

- Assess their readiness,

- Set a date, and

- Specify the required documentation and provide information on arrangements.

When assessment of readiness indicates problems (which occur in approximately 5% of the couples that you see), the following things should be done.

- Decide on the necessity of refusal or delay,

- Tell them why,

- Suggest the forms of help that you and others can provide,

- Deal with their feelings and with those of their parents,

- Arrange special handling, and

- Offer avenues of appeal.

Session Two: First Follow-Up

Session Two should be devoted to processing the couple's marriage education experience.

- Obtain their reactions,

- Personalize the various content areas to their needs,

- Discuss any questions more fully if necessary,

- Discuss more deeply the sacramental meaning of marriage and life in the Church, and

- Explain the options they have in designing the liturgy for the wedding ceremony.

Session Three: Second Follow-Up

- Finalize and collect all necessary documents,

- Agree on the liturgical service and vows in detail,

- Coordinate all arrangements, including interfaith service, priest/friend celebrant, etc,

- Set a time for the rehearsal,

- Ask the couple to evaluate the premarriage preparation program, and

- Talk about plans for strengthening their relationship in the future.

Figure 1 (see pages 40-41) illustrates the flow of activity from promulgation of policy on premarriage preparation to initial contact with engaged couples and through to completion of the premarriage sessions and the wedding.

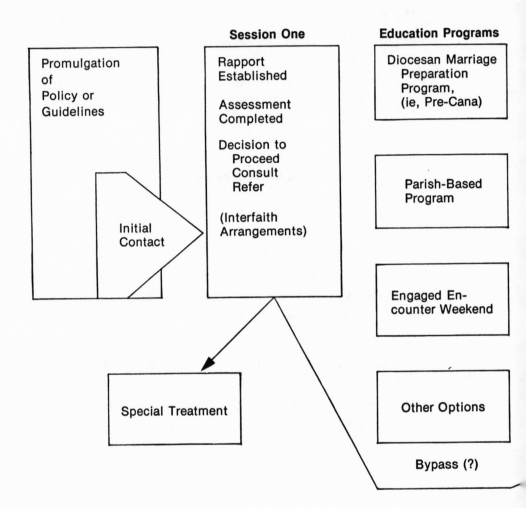

Session One

Education Programs

Promulgation
of
Policy or
Guidelines

Initial
Contact

Rapport
Established

Assessment
Completed

Decision to
 Proceed
 Consult
 Refer

(Interfaith
Arrangements)

Diocesan Marriage
Preparation
Program,
(ie, Pre-Cana)

Parish-Based
Program

Engaged En-
counter Weekend

Special Treatment

Other Options

Bypass (?)

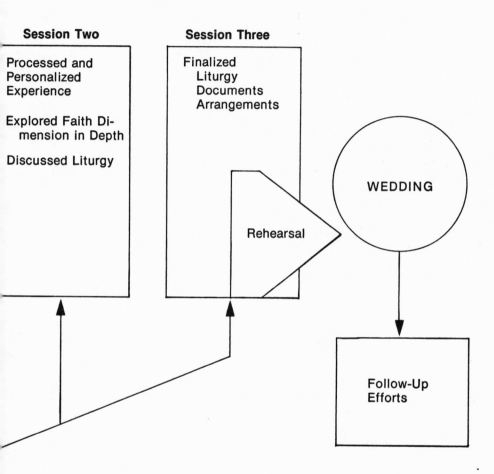

Figure 1.

Visual display of the activity involved in premarriage preparation process, from promulgation of policy to initial contact with engaged couples and through to the education program, follow-up sessions, and wedding.

6

**Session
One**
—
Initial Contact

The Couple Calls

Usually, couples who wish to set up an appointment to discuss marriage plans will contact the rectory by phone. Most often, because it is her parish, the woman will place the call. If the caller asks for a particular priest, and he is available, fine. If the couple asks for no one in particular, the secretary should connect the caller with one of the priests on duty. If the caller requests a priest who is unavailable at the moment, the secretary should take the message and have the priest return the call as soon as possible.

If the secretary is able to make appointments for the priests, she should not make an appointment for a premarriage interview unless she is certain that the priest can spend at least an hour with the couple during the first session. Further, the secretary should never reserve a date or time for the wedding. If the couple requests a date that is at least four-to-six months in the future, however, the secretary can let the caller know whether it is available, but she should also caution that the couple must talk with the priest before the date can be reserved.

If the priest is available and answers the phone he should follow the same guidelines and also let the couple know that he will be happy to help them plan their marriage. It is helpful during this first discussion to display interest in their plans, in the prospective partner, and in the length and duration of their relationship and engagement. Such interest establishes a friendly rapport and helps you move toward a good working relationship during marriage preparation.

After establishing an appointment time, the priest should tell the couple to plan to spend at least an hour at the first session. If the question of a wedding date arises, and the date they have selected is at least four months in the future, the same course of action is appropriate. That is, the priest might indicate that he will put a tentative hold on the date, but that he also must talk with them before he can make a definite commitment to reserving a date for their wedding. He should also advise the caller that the parish has a formal marriage preparation procedure that he will explain in detail during the first session.

The Couple's Fear of the Rectory

For a variety of reasons, some couples are not apprehensive about the first interview. However, do not underestimate the anxiety with which some engaged couples face the ordeal of entering the rectory. For some, the rectory is a place of mystery or judgment. Many of them will enter the rectory for the first time in their lives; they do not know quite what to expect. Some resent having to appear before the priest—a legalism they can barely tolerate. They wish merely to get done with the business without hassle.

The worst mistake a priest can make is to not be aware of these anxieties; the second mistake is to think that he can dispel them within thirty seconds with only a smile. Often, much work is entailed just to win the couples over and help them open up so that productive dialogue can occur.

Greeting

Make certain that the couple is greeted warmly by whomever opens the door. If you will not be available immediately, make sure that they are seated in a comfortable, attractive waiting area. If you are detained for more than a few minutes, someone should explain that you will be delayed and let the couple know how long they can expect to wait. Nothing increases anxiety more than a prolonged, unexplained wait, particularly if the couple already felt threatened before they arrived.

Ambience and All That

First impressions are important, and the room in which you meet is important also. Although you might have limited control over the setting, it is wise to think of the following considerations. That is, soft lamplight is much more conducive to a relaxed atmosphere than cold flourescent lighting; comfortable chairs will be appreciated; and good colors, attractive pictures, a rug, and plants add immeasurably to the atmosphere.

A minimum of office equipment and machines is advisable. Consider not using a desk. If you prefer a desk, or if you meet in your office and the desk cannot be removed, sit in front of the desk so that it becomes a common work area rather than a barrier.

Some priests suggest having coffee or refreshments available. Offering food or drink is a sign of friendship and hospitality; eating together has deep, positive, symbolic meaning. People share food with those whom they trust, know, and like. Sharing food can eliminate a feeling of strangeness or the fear that you and the couple are adversaries.

Establishing Rapport

Rapport is a blend of mutual respect, openness, understanding, trust, and emotional affinity. Establishing rapport does not happen immediately or automatically, especially if people are anxious and tense. Your greeting, opening remarks, and conversational approaches are important. Do not be afraid to engage in small talk and chat away some of the hour: It might be the most important thing that you do during the first session.

Expressions of warmth, empathy, and reassurance and attempts at informality or humor are invaluable. Telling brief stories about yourself, other couples, and the problems you encountered during the week make you seem more human. The fact that you feel comfortable about sharing thoughts and feelings will encourage the couple to open up.

Questions about their plans and arrangements can communicate your understanding of their situation. References to the anxieties and apprehensions that they might be experiencing after their decision to marry (and discussion of how normal such jitters are), also increase empathy and enhance your acceptability and credibility. If the couple is eager and confident, you might not need to spend as much time establishing rapport, but you can begin to reinforce their enthusiasm. Whatever you do, keep tuned in to what they are saying and how they are responding.

Opening Approaches

"Tell me a little about yourselves," is an acceptable opening which helps the priest evaluate the feelings, anxieties, and personalities of the couple. Some priests like to ask the question and see which partner responds first and how the couple proceeds. Others have a number of specific questions that will cue the couple. (See Appendix B for a list of some of these questions and cues.)

Some priests have found that questions like Where did you go to school? What kind of work do you do? and Where will you be living? are among the least threatening to couples. Others suggest that it is useful to look for common ground at this stage. If you know anything about their school, faculty, teams, courses of study, you can contribute in a positive, friendly fashion to the conversation. If you are knowledgeable about the type of work that the couple does, you can ask leading questions to display interest, to encourage the couple to elaborate on nonthreatening topics about which they have knowledge, and to stimulate conversation.

When you have proceeded in this direction comfortably for a period of time, you have one or two options for handling the rest of the first session. You can continue to get to know the couple, encourage them to tell their story in more detail, and gradually focus on topics more closely related to their attitudes on marriage. Or, some priests prefer to shift gears, establish the agenda, and give the couple an overview of what to expect during the rest of the session and throughout the premarriage preparation process. Remember, the couple has an agenda which should also be considered and their participation should be encouraged.

If you choose the latter option, you might consider moving directly into discussion as informally as possible: "Let me talk with you a bit to let you know where I'm coming from and what to expect during the remainder of our time together tonight. I'd also like to let you know about the rest of the marriage preparation program."

Then you should move into a discussion that both provides an orientation to the premarriage program and presents the concept of Christian love. The couple should also get a sense of your support for them and their decision to marry. Several suggested approaches to this orientation follow.

§

You Are Important and So Is Marriage. As you know, divorce rates continue to escalate, and every divorce involves hurt and personal heartache. Some say that marriage, as an institution, is on its way out. Well, the Church does not believe that. But, it does believe that couples deserve all the help they can get to build a happy and satisfying marriage. So, although I want to help you make the wedding day itself happy and memorable, we will focus primarily on discussions about your married life.

§

Stress. The weeks before marriage can be hectic and stressful—a veritable zoo sometimes. One of the reasons that the Church requires a four-month preparation period before the wedding date is to assure sufficient time amidst these hectic plans to explore and reflect on your relationship and the meaning of marriage.

§

New Beginning. Marriage can be a new beginning for both of you. It's rather like pulling up stakes and heading for another part of the country, forgetting the past, taking on a new identity, and beginning life anew—ready to be whatever you want to be. I don't mean that you won't take your personality traits, your strengths and weaknesses, and faults and foibles into marriage with you. I do mean that you enter into a passage time, a time of dreams, a time of dedication and resolutions to be better and happier than ever, because you have someone who loves you very much to support and challenge you.

Engagement is your first season of love. Don't waste it arguing about invitations and menus. Make your engagement a time to deepen trust and communication and to talk about your dreams, goals, and fears.

§

The Program. In general, the premarriage program will go like this: We will spend this session getting to know one another better and checking out whether any problems exist or any areas of special interest should be explored. I'll tell you what kinds of documents you'll need, and I'll also tell you where to get all the practical information you need about arranging for flowers and music, etc.

I will discuss the kinds of marriage education programs that are available and ask you to choose the one you wish to attend. After you have completed the program, we will get together for two more sessions. During the session after the program, we will discuss your reactions to it, and determine if any topics need further elaboration or explanation. At that session I will also discuss the Christian dimension of marriage and explore your feelings about it. During the final session, we will wrap things up, make certain all papers are in order, and plan the wedding liturgy so that it is personal and meaningful to you and a celebration for your friends and relatives.

§

The Church and Marriage. Let me finish by saying that, as a priest, I speak for a special kind of marrying. The Church is, in the final analysis, those people who believe in and live our Lord's message of love. Priests are those in the Church community assigned to keeping Christ's teaching alive and fresh. To do so, we must challenge and inspire people.

We believe in Christ when he said, "If you would find your life, you must lay it down." This principle, which clashes head on with so many beliefs in our self-centered society, is at the heart of Christ's teaching. He tells us to become, to grow, to mature, and to find meaning in life by taking the risk of forgetting yourselves and loving others. And risky it is. For, as you most likely know, when we drop our defenses and invest our faith and trust in another, we become vulnerable, and we risk being hurt and betrayed. But risking ourselves in love is the basic dynamic of personal growth, and Church teaching on marriage is rooted in the law of love.

The Church does not propose exclusive, indissoluble marriage to restrict or limit couples. The Church proposes such marriages because it fully believes that those who accept such a covenant, those who understand, believe, and firmly commit themselves to be together forever will be drawn, enticed, and challenged by love to live their lives richly and fully--and be an inspiration and a symbol (sacrament, if you will) to each other and to all around them. But that is a heavy concept, and we will come back to it again later and try to explore it in greater detail.

Okay, that's my agenda. I would like you to comment, ask questions, and tell me what *you* want to consider or discuss during the time we spend together. What is your agenda?

§

It is important to give the couple due opportunity to comment, ask questions, and discuss whatever is on their minds. Don't create the impression that this is *your* performance or they will become passive and wait for you to get on with the next act.

After the preceding orientation, you can continue to get to know the couple by suggesting questions or topics for discussion. Or you might take them through the prenuptial questionnaire, which will help raise any issues or canonical problems that should be confronted early on. Some priests discuss many of the items on the questionnaire (such as family data, religion, previous marriages, religious practices, etc.) during the general discussion. The act of filling out forms is thus more brief and informal.

Some prefer to separate the couple and, while one partner is working on the formal questionnaire, the other fills out an informal questionnaire that incorporates some of the questions in Appendix B. Comparing each partner's answers to the informal questionnaire often is an excellent way to initiate discussion. Whatever your approach, you are now moving to the heart of the assessment process.

Assessment of Readiness to Marry

One of the most important tasks in Session One is to assess the couple's readiness to marry. How will you do this? First, be clear about what should be assessed, next, reflect on the criteria that you will use.

What is Being Assessed?

Assess the couple's *present state* of maturity, considering age, experience, and life circumstances. Do they have positive patterns of development as persons?

Assess their *potential*, asking the following questions. Do they have potential for personal growth in responsibility, wisdom, and selflessness? Do they have potential for relating to each other well, with caring, communication, and creativity? Do they have potential for building a life together which will be intimate, rewarding, and bonding? Do they have potential for parenting with grace and humor?

Do they have the capacity, understanding, intention, realism, and idealism to commit themselves to the long adventure that is marriage? Do they have a faith vision (or at least the beginnings of one) that enables them to see their marriage as inspired by and representing Christ's invitation to total love?

NOTE: If your answer is a *ringing yes* to all of the above, marry them and canonize them immediately!

The assessment is NOT looking for perfection. It is looking for ordinary mortals who have a dream, who care for each other, who are without inhibiting defects, and who are willing to try.

Criteria* for Assessing Readiness to Marry

Upon being asked how his wife was, James Thurber, the humorist, had a classic and wise response, "Compared to what?" The criteria used to assess anything influences a person's evaluation, of course. Among umpires, a one-eyed man is a pariah, although in the world of the blind, he could be king!

What criteria should a priest apply in assessing a couple's readiness and potential for marriage? Some criteria clearly signal impediments and dangers that warrant refusal or delay. However, when it comes to more subtle and positive predictors of success, no criteria exist that are infallible, and some would say that none exist that are wholly adequate.

Nevertheless, some criteria exist that are worth using. Often, a priest will feel "right" about a couple, and if pressed to explain might say something like, "They are serious, sensible, sincere, and seem to understand each other. They are reasonably religious, able to handle themselves, and seem to know what they are doing." These are good criteria. Breaking the set into components, we offer the following criteria.

---

*Pooling experience to refine the criteria and to name several others, such as flexibility, emotional stability, honesty, compatibility, and shared values, would be a major service to those involved in premarriage ministry.

Serious and somewhat knowledgeable about marriage. You will be able to determine this if it is clear that they have had discussions and made realistic plans about work, life careers, economics, where to live, goals, sex, children, possible problem areas, etc.

Committed to succeed. The strong intention to "make it work" has, in most longitudinal studies, been one of the most consistent predictors of marital success. You will be able to determine this if the couple has constructive answers to such questions as, "What would you do if several years from now your relationship ran into serious, unforeseen problems?" or, "Can you see yourself sacrificing some of your freedom, ambitions, or interests to make your marriage work?"

Self insight. Do each of the partners have the capacity to reflect on their basic personality traits, and is each aware of how he or she functions in and responds to stress, disappointment, confusion, etc? You will be able to determine this if they give sensible, thoughtful answers to such questions as, "What do you believe is your greatest weakness and/or strength as a marriage partner?" You will also be able to determine this if you see evidence that they have learned from previous mistakes and do not repeat these mistakes over and over again.

Communication. Do they consider communication important? Do they have some skills in communication? Do they take time to communicate with one another?

You will be able to determine this if they have developed enough mutual trust to begin to reveal some of their fears, weaknesses, and dreams to each other. The quality of their exchange with one another during the interview will also help you determine how they communicate.

Openness to the religious dimension of marriage. You will be able to determine this when:

- they themselves make the decision to have a church wedding and view it as something more than a social custom;

- they provide the beginnings of an acceptable answer to the question "How, in your view, does religious (sacramental) marriage differ from others?";

- they are reasonably conscientious in the practice of their faith; and

- they seem sincerely open to using the occasion of their marriage as a new start if they have neglected their faith life in the past.

Sense of responsibility. A sense of responsibility in the couple will be evidenced by the following:

- ability to accept the consequences of their actions and decisions;

- direction in their work, careers, or school plans, as opposed to drifting, confusion, and a record spotted with frequent job changes;

- ability to finish what they start;

- no major tendencies to blame others for their problems and failures;

- involvement in civic, charitable, or volunteer activities; and

- concern for a liturgy that would be meaningful to their parents, relatives, and elders, as well as their peers.

Love and the capacity for intimacy. Love and the capacity for intimacy will be evidenced by the following:

- warmth, concern, humor, positive interplay, and display of respect, empathy, compassion, and willingness to enter the other's world and let the other in theirs; and
- a minimal amount of self-centeredness and tendency to carry the discussion on the relationship and marriage.

Alerts

Alerts are situations or circumstances that often warrant further discussion and deeper investigation. Several are discussed briefly on the following pages.

Drift. If a couple has been courting seriously for a long time and/or has been engaged for many months, why do they want to marry now? What precipitated the decision? What delayed them before? Are they drifting into the inevitable without confronting the decision and its implications?

Patchwork. Has the couple broken the relationship or engagement more than once? If yes, have the problems that caused the breakup been confronted and resolved? Or have they been ignored and covered up?

The Absolute Need to Marry. If one partner were to leave or be eaten by a tiger, would the other be completely devastated and unable to go on? Marriage is an adult vocation for people who want to enrich and complete their lives; for those who can share, give to, and experience with another. Marrige is not a panacea for neurotic needs, a refuge for the dependent, or a hiding place for the weak.

Rebounders. Has one or both partners recently come from a traumatic relationship or broken engagement, and is he or she embarking on the marriage to "show" someone or to prove his or her ability to attract a mate?

Time Together. Sometimes, the time assigned to the length of the relationship or engagement can be deceiving. The couple might say that they have been "serious for over a year." However, she has been away at school, and he has a job that requires frequent travel. They might actually have spent very little time together that was not at parties, events, and other social activities.

Therapist. If one of the partners has a problem, such as alcohol, irresponsibility, gambling, drugs, instability, a violent temper, etc; and the other (usually the woman) is convinced that her loving and caring will change all that after the wedding, this situation must be discussed. There is still truth in the old adage that "if he or she will not change to get you, he will not change to keep you." The priest should watch carefully to determine whether a psychological need to have a partner be dependent exists in the partner who is therapist.

Age. The failure rate in marriage between partners who are under 21 is over 50%, and the younger they are, the higher the rate. If pregnancy is involved, the failure rate may be as high as 75-80%. The reasons are obvious. Because they are young, many of these couples lack the experience, maturity, interpersonal skills, and a reasonable economic basis for their life together. Further, they might have very few marketable skills at such a young age. At this age, couples are also more susceptible to the need to escape, to boredom factors, and to the "lemming" syndrome. They might want to get away from home or school; "give their lives a sense of direction;" "all" of their friends are getting married. And so they use marriage as a solution to their identity crises.

Age Differential. If the age differential is more than six or seven years, this factor might be worth probing, particularly if one of the partners is very young.

Class Distinction. As a concept, class distinction is taboo in the minds of Americans who are shaped by the melting pot myth. But, if one partner is well-educated, used to money, highly verbal, ambitious, and imbued with certain social interests, spending habits, lifestyle preferences, etc; while the other is the complete opposite, the situation merits discussion. An informal rule of thumb that some marriage counselors like to use is the answer to the question "Will he or she take pride in displaying, introducing, and being associated with this spouse?"

Premarital Sex. One of the most unfortunate results of premarital sexual involvement is marriage that is based on fear or guilt only. Mistaking erotic experience for love, or feeling guilty or inextricably bound or committed because they have "gone all the way," some couples short-circuit the getting to know you process, blink at problems, and leap into marriage.

Unresponsiveness. If the couple appears hostile or un-cooperative, if their answers are monosyllabic, if you cannot engage them in any discussion despite your best efforts; and if they seem to barely tolerate the proceedings, this is a real danger signal. Before you assess them too negatively, however, make another attempt to break through and discover the roots of their feelings. To be candid is probably the best approach. "I get the feeling that you really resent being here, and that makes me uneasy. Can you tell me why you and I are having such a difficult time communicating? Am I turning you off? Are there other things that we should be talking about? Do you feel that this whole process is an imposition? What are you thinking?

One Less than Eager. A priest frequently will sense that one of the partners has taken charge of the courtship and preparations, while the other is "along for the ride." When you suspect that the less involved partner would "cut and run" if he or she could do so without hurting the other or losing face, you might talk with the less eager partner alone. Although you might talk with them both separately as a matter of course, try not to give them the sense that something unusual is occurring. Use an introductory phrase such as "I'd like to spend a little time with each of you separately now." Give one of them something to read or fill out while talking to the other partner.

Again, candor is the best approach with the less than eager partner. "I feel a bit uncomfortable about this situation because I sense that you are uneasy and that you are not completely settled about things. How do you feel about the way things are going? Do you have any problems about your readiness to proceed? Do you think some things should be discussed further among the three of us? If you could postpone the wedding for a while, would you?

Reaching Conclusions

In the vast majority of instances, your assessment of a couple will be positive. A wedding date will be set, and emphasis will shift to using the time before the wedding to deepen their relationship and their understanding of Christian marriage. Certain situations will become clear during the first session as you use your skills to interpret behaviors and apply the criteria discussed earlier. Some typical situations which you might encounter and some suggestions for handling them are listed.

The Clear Negative

If an obvious impediment, such as a previous bond or a serious incapacity, has surfaced and necessitates refusal or delay, meet the problem immediately. "I think we have a problem that we just can't get around, etc." The couple may well be disappointed, but unless they are wholly lacking in information about the Church's marriage requirements, they will have suspected that their situation was questionable and/or impossible. Your judgment will not come as a total shock.

What they need is for you to be honest. "I think it highly unlikely that you will ever be able to marry in the Church." Or, they need your expert help and guidance. "To rectify this situation (assuming that it can be rectified), we would go through XX procedure, which would entail XYZ steps, and might take as long as Q." Once they know the whys and wherefores, how they must proceed, how you can help, and if you can help, the decision about how to proceed is theirs.

The Marginal Couple

Some couples, perhaps those who are very young, not terribly interested in a religious ceremony, or under family pressure to marry "in the traditional way," might just be "shopping." One or both partners might have had psychology and sociology courses in college, know all about transactional analysis and matrilineal family systems, and absolutely refuse to involve themselves in any further marriage preparation. In such a situation, a 'turndown' or delay most likely will not be devastating. The real challenge is to break through their indifference of pseudo-sophistication, to get under their skin, make them understand the seriousness of marriage and its religious dimension, and help them change their attitudes.

The Unsuspecting Unready

The unsuspecting unready is the eager couple that presumes everything is fine. If, after your interview, you are seriously inclined to refuse or delay the marriage, then you probably are in one of two states of mind:

- You have uncovered and can state one or more specific significant reasons for your conclusions.

- You have a diffuse negative impression ("gut feeling") about one or both of the partners or the couple's attitude or relationship.

If the first is true, and your reasons are clear, then it might be best to review the area of difficulty. You might even suggest that certain things trouble you. Further discussion might put the matter in a new light and permit the wedding to proceed. If, however, further discussion confirms your reservations, it will also alert the couple to what comes next.

If the latter situation exists and you have only a gut feeling, it is *your responsibility* to analyze and clarify your thoughts and reactions and perhaps discuss and probe some areas again until you *state your objections clearly, weigh their severity, and educe evidence to support them.*

A desk pad or clipboard on which you can jot notes intermittently to help you organize your thoughts might be a good idea, particularly for less experienced counselors who might feel swamped by the amount of data that surfaces in an interview.

In any case, if you are firm in your decision to refuse or delay the wedding, you should tell the couple as clearly, precisely, and gently as possible. Listen seriously and openly to any rebuttal or clarifications they offer. If you decide to hold to your decision, recommend the most fitting remedy possible, which might be one or more of the following:

- Another discussion about what the concerns are, after the three of you have had the opportunity to think about or consult on the matter.

- Attendance at a premarriage education program followed by reevaluation.

- A specified waiting period for them to get to know each other better, reconsider their decision, etc.

- Consultation with a professional—physician, psychologist, lawyer, debt counselor, etc., whom you will help them find.

- A session with a Catholic Family Consultation Service, if available, or some other agency—possibly to be followed by individual or group counseling, which you will help arrange.

If they are inclined not to agree with the course of action that you recommend, further discussion about its value is in order. Or, you might suggest that they take a few days to consider your decision and discuss it privately. In any case, keep the door open. Suggest that you will be in touch and will follow up. Offer to help explain the situation to their parents, who might react to the decision to delay with glee or rage.

Finally, suggest that they have *avenues of appeal* through another priest or parish or through the chancery. Conclude with a recap of what has been decided and a clear agreement about who will do what, and when.

The Premarital Inventory (PMI)

The *Premarital Inventory* is a tool that has been used widely throughout the U.S. as an aid to the priest in his efforts to identify strengths and weaknesses in a couple's relationship.

The *PMI* is a carefully structured inventory that asks couples to identify levels of agreement or disagreement on ten dimensions of marriage—children; finances; inlaws; communication; interests and activities; marriage readiness; personal adjustment; religion and philosophy; role adjustment and sexuality. From the couple's responses to the inventory, a profile can be drawn of their communication level.

Strengths of the PMI

- An effective foundation/guideline for worthwhile conversation with the engaged couple.

- Leads the couple gently into an examination of their true feelings.

- Assists the priest in his final evaluation of a couple's readiness for marriage.

Weaknesses and Cautionary Note

- *PMI* is not a test, and you should not expect it to predict the potential success of a marriage.

- A time commitment is involved in administering the *PMI*. You will need at least 35 minutes to complete the inventory, time to score and graph the results, and time for the essential discussion that should follow.

The *Premarital Inventory* can be obtained by writing to the following address.

BESS ASSOCIATES
Box 4148
4700 S. Poplar
Casper, Wyoming 81604

Cost (includes mailing) $6.15. Kit inclues 2 questionnaires; 1 overlay; 1 table; 2 answer sheets; 1 graph; and 2 data sheets.

Praying with the Couple

Prayer can be an important dimension of your work with couples. Prayer can touch us and evoke faith in ways that mere words of explanation and discussion cannot. Spend the last few moments of a session with a couple listening to or reading a passage from Scripture that reflects the biblical view of married life. (One young man was amazed to find that Paul's letter on love to the Corinthians was from the Bible; he thought it was too good to come from the Bible.) Invite the couple to mention their hopes, aspirations, and dreams in prayer and include what they will be praying for on their wedding day.

Use a reading from the Wedding Liturgy itself in these moments of prayer. This will help familiarize the couple with the ceremony and put them in touch with what they will be celebrating and praying for on their wedding day.

Reading together a prayer of blessing for the engaged can also be a good prayer experience. Although you might feel uncomfortable suggesting closing prayers to a couple, please try to overcome your discomfort. Couples expect us to *be* who we are—people of faith and people of prayer. (See example page 68).

Prayer for the Engaged

God our Father, in your own good care and wisdom we have come to know each other. We have come to discover something of the mystery of each other. We have come to love each other. Pour out your blessings on (name) whom I want to love for the rest of my life; blessings for safety, for strength, for joy.

Help us, as we form a family together, to find a new way to love the families where we have been loved and nourished till now. In these hectic weeks and afterwards, help us laugh when small plans don't work out, and make us willing to support each other in real problems.

Let us stay always secure in one another, secure in you and in prayer. Grace our relationship with the gift of your Holy Spirit, so that, day by day, our affection may grow into self-sacrifice, our passion into deep human care, and our warm feeling into lasting commitment. Bring to fulfillment the wonder of your ways which you have begun to reveal to us. We pray this through Christ our Lord.

7

Sessions Two and Three —

Follow-Up

Although the priest should be aware of distinct objectives for sessions two and three, both sessions will be discussed together because they are follow-up sessions whose content overlaps somewhat.

These sessions provide follow-up to the first "assessment" session and, hopefully, to the couple's premarriage education experience. The wedding liturgy, their future life together, and the religious dimension of marriage are all topics which most likely will be discussed in both sessions.

Rapport and Ambience

Couples may still be very nervous or anxious when they come to the second and third sessions. Anything you can do to provide a warm atmosphere and an open attitude will alleviate the pressure they feel.

Your mental preparedness is also important. Look over any notes you might have made during your first encounter with the couple. Review your conversation. Remember who they are; get their names right. Spending a few minutes in preparation will ensure a smooth start in these sessions.

Although certain tasks must be accomplished, also work toward deepening your relationship with the couple (and their relationship with each other,) by engaging them in worthwhile conversation, listening to what they have to say about any of a wide range of topics that relate to their marriage. You can discuss anything that will improve their communication. The topics will vary with each couple. With some you might emphasize faith commitment; with others you might discuss finances, children, etc.

And, although to focus on their future is important, take time to discuss the here and now. Be aware that the weeks before the wedding are laden with stress and tension as well as excitement and joy. Invite them to share their tension and joy with you. Ask them how things are going in their lives and with their plans, jobs, and their relationship with each other and their families.

The priest's role is that of friend, teacher, and guide, not psychologist. These two sessions should be looked upon as an opportunity for ministry and catechesis, with the priest helping people to look at marriage and the Church and to learn and grow.

The Follow-Up

You presume that when the engaged couple comes for the second session they already have attended a marriage preparation program. You should, of course, ascertain that they attended the program, but more importantly, you should assess their reactions to the program and to the content or ideas presented. Their reactions will provide meat for discussion and should earmark areas that require explanation or exploration.

Couples will not always be willing to participate in the discussion we suggest. One of the best ways to ferret out their true reactions is to ask them to describe the program they attended. Their "description" should at least provide a hint of their opinion and get the ball rolling, so to speak.

Simple questions are therefore in order. Where did you go? Who directed the conference? What were the presentations like? These questions are much more likely to spark conversation than What topics would you like to discuss further? Do you have any questions about the material presented in the program? Many couples would probably answer "no," and you would not have assessed their needs. Let them describe their experience while you listen for any negative or confused feelings or areas worth pursuing.

Religious Dimension

In the second session, discuss the religious dimension of marriage (see Appendix C, "Notes Toward a Rationale for Christian Marriage"). How you present this to the couple will, of course, vary from couple to couple and will depend on whether they are both Catholic; whether they were educated in Catholic schools; whether they are active or borderline Catholics; and what their education level is. These and other factors will influence the depth and breadth of your discussion. If a couple appears to be disinterested, it might be that they have limited knowledge of the religious dimension of faith.

Because this stage of marriage preparation can be awkward, proceed gently and thoughtfully. Be in touch with your own emotions regarding the religious dimension of marriage; your emotions can make or break your explanation. However, don't overlook the religious dimension of marriage; couples expect us to be who we say we are. They *expect* you to regard marriage as holy and sacramental. You might begin by saying something similar to the following.

§

You probably know that marriage is considered a sacrament in the Catholic Church. Although such a statement is made readily, it might not be understood or appreciated quite so readily. Put simply, marriage is a sacrament because it is an expression of God's love and grace. In marriage, when you pledge yourselves to one another and live through that commitment, the very nature of that commitment makes your marriage in the church special and holy.

§

Every marriage involves commitment, but commitment in Christian marriage is not the type of commitment in which a contract exists, with rules and conditions that nullify the contract if broken. If you will, Christian marriage is an unconditional guarantee, for a lifetime. It's a guarantee made in good faith to be faithful to the other person, no matter what. In religious jargon we use the word "covenant" when speaking of the guarantee. A convenant is a solemn, holy, and special promise and you make it to each other with God's help. You are not merely 'making a deal' with each other; you are making a holy agreement that requires love, courage, and more than a little help from your friend, Jesus Christ.

§

We make a 'big deal' about this because it is a big deal—the biggest you will ever be involved in. When you make this commitment, you make it for the rest of your lives. Naming marriage a sacrament is a way of confirming what it already is—an event so important in magnitude and scope that God's involvement in your pledge shines forth through your love, courage, and faith.

§

You can illustrate the holiness of marriage by using concrete examples of the Christian aspect of marriage, ie, forgiveness, self-sacrifice, and unconditional love (loving the unlovable). Use gospel stories such as the Prodigal Son and the Good Samaritan to illustrate these concepts. This type of discussion will help the couple focus not only on the marriage pledge but on the future consequences of that pledge in their lives and on deepening their understanding of Christianity.

Liturgy Planning

To merely provide a couple with a sheet of options for their wedding liturgy is not sufficient. Good liturgy planning should take place in three stages, two of which will be accomplished with you during the second and third sessions and one of which the couple will handle alone.

Stage One. Stage one of liturgy preparation should occur at the second session. Included in this stage is preparing the couple for arranging their liturgy; providing them with necessary information (eg, the actual prayer choices, rules and regulations); and giving them guidance and encouragement, as well as explanations of the liturgy.

Take time to convey to the couple the meaning of different parts of the wedding liturgy. Praying with the couple is an approach, mentioned earlier, which deserves repeating in this context. At the end of each session, read a passage or two from the liturgy, which will familiarize the couple with a few choices and develop their understanding of particular sections of the liturgy.

Give the couple something that provides them with standard choices and a brief explanation of each liturgical section of the wedding ceremony. (One booklet that we recommend is available from Buckley Publications, Inc; Chicago, and is titled "Celebrate Your Wedding Day." The publication is designed to assist couples to understand the

liturgy and make choices that meet their individual tastes.)
Another tool is to give the couple a blank sheet on which
they can indicate their choices. They can fill the sheet out
and bring it to the final session, or they can fill it out with
you at the final session.

Let the couple know that they can and should involve
family, attendants, etc., in the liturgy. You might quickly
review the points in the liturgy and ceremony where this
type of involvement fits and is helpful. Ask them to decide
early who will be involved so that confusion can be avoided
at the rehearsal.

At this point, you could explain what portions of the
ceremony they can compose themselves and how to do it.
Emphasize that originality is not as important as meaning.
Let them know what you prefer and whether you will allow
any other reading selections.

This stage of liturgy planning should involve your assessment of the type of couple selecting the liturgy, ie, indif-
ferent (some are); conservative (want the whole thing in
Latin with Gregorian chant); far-out (balloons and bread-
sticks for all); and/or any variations of the same between
these extremes.

Some can be so timid and respectful that you will have to
help and encourage them to make choices. Others might be
a little mystified by the responsibility, in which case you
will have to explain further. Still others might be defiant
and expecting a fight, in which case you will have to be
openminded and bide your time for the opportunity to guide
and direct.

Music is frequently a point of tension and contention.
Couples are quite likely to have made decisions about music
before they began to plan the liturgy. They have favorite
songs in mind, and dreams of the perfect wedding often in-

clude those songs. Young people love music; be sympathetic and recognize that music is probably very important to them. When presented with the wide range of available choices, most couples will be able to select music that is pleasing to all concerned. Again, you have to walk the fine line between encouraging creativity and personalization in wedding music and discouraging the temptation to organize a musical extravaganza.

Ask them to consult with the parish organist or music director. It is really best to put the decisions about music in the hands of a professional (if at all possible), allowing the professional to have the final say on what is usable or acceptable. This lets you off the hook a little bit too.

It should be stated clearly by you or the parish musician that the purpose of music in liturgy is to help people pray and that music should be useful pastorally in that it has the assembled congregation in mind—if not for their participation, then at least for their appreciation. Music should also be fitting liturgically, ie, suitable to the service as part of the worship.

NOTE: A booklet titled "Handbook of Church Music for Weddings," available from the Liturgy Training Program of the Archdiocese of Chicago, offers many choices and would be a handy reference for you, the music director, and the engaged couple.

Stage Two. In Stage Two, the couple discusses the liturgy and music in private and makes a decision, perhaps creating some of their own material for parts of the liturgy. Ideally, this stage should occur between your second and third sessions with the couple, not during a fifteen minute period when you leave them alone in the rectory. Suggest that they allow enough time to at least glance at all readings so that they make a reasoned choice.

At this time, include a visit and consultation with the parish music director and other musicians.

Stage Three. Stage Three occurs at your third session with the couple (or at whatever session you have with them before the wedding rehearsal). The couple might present a sheet of selections to you at the third session or fill out the "official" copy of their liturgy plan at this time. Any original portions (vows, etc.) and any nonstandard reading selections should be reviewed and discussed carefully.

If the couple has hired their own musicians, make certain you ask them who the musicians are, the type of music and type of instruments they play, etc. Discuss where the musicians will stand during the ceremony and whether they will need any special equipment from the parish (such as microphones, chairs, etc). Discuss arrangements for letting the musicians into the Church to set up early.

Take care of all loose ends. Find out what the couple plans for flowers and other decorations. Be as helpful as you can with suggestions on how everything might best be expedited. Ask about the wedding party, the processional, the kiss of peace, etc. What about contacting the other officiating minister or providing housing for a visiting priest? A brief mention of each of these and written decisions can alleviate confusion at the rehearsal and wedding. It is clear that planning is important to avoid last minute scrambles and disappointments.

Set a time for the rehearsal (see page 81 for a discussion of the rehearsal itself).

Paperwork

Take care of the canonical papers and any other important paperwork during the third session. Although the substance of the canonical papers should be covered in the first session, don't involve the couple with the papers themselves at that time. We should avoid giving the impression that we are concerned only with forms.

On occasion, a couple or one partner will balk at responding to the questions or signing the papers. Simply explain that signing these papers reflects the seriousness of their intentions and their readiness for marriage. Point out that signing one's name is a universal symbol of responsibility and good faith and an accepted means of clarifying the importance of an act or deed.

If they claim that the questions are intrusive or provocative, you might remind them gently of the Church's responsibility for marriage. To agree to perform an official act (ie, witness the marriage), the Church needs assurance that the ceremony does indeed represent true commitment made in good faith. And, don't forget to remind them to get a marriage license!

Conclusion

Sessions two and three provide the opportunity to enrich the couple's premarital preparation experience and their marital life. Let them know that you will be glad to help them at any time throughout their marriage—during joy and sorrows, strain and stress. Invite them to become active in the Church community; inform them of the types of programs available for couples their age. And, finally, ask them to evaluate the marriage preparation experience—either through discussion, or, more formally on a prepared evaluation form. Give them the opportunity to voice their opinions, any complaints, and offer suggestions.

Rehearsal Notes

Admittedly, the rehearsal often is a burdensome task for the priest—a hassle, a boring exercise, inglorious at best. But, it is a very exciting event for the couple, the family, and friends. They are almost there—their dreams are about to come true, emotions are running high, everyone is uptight. So—sensitivity is important. Look upon the half hour of rehearsal as an opportunity to meet the family and establish a rapport that will enhance the warm atmosphere of the wedding.

Keep explanations simple; the rehearsal should not be longer than the wedding. Any discussions should have occurred during your liturgy planning sessions with the couple. The rehearsal is not the time to decide who would be the best reader or how the vows will be worded, but a walk-through of what has been planned already. Make certain that any non-Catholics in the wedding party are aware of everything that is going on.

You might start off with a liturgy reading to set the proper mood for rehearsal. Another short prayer or reading at the completion of rehearsal can help focus on the true meaning of the ceremony.

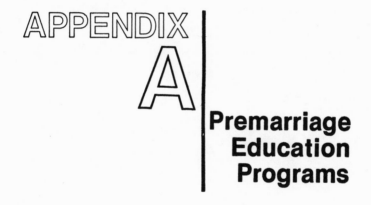

APPENDIX

A

**Premarriage
Education
Programs**

Diocesan programming for premarriage preparation varies widely. One diocese might have structured, regularly scheduled programs with printed materials and a corps of trained leaders. Another might rely entirely on the parish to fulfill the task of premarriage preparation. Whatever the case, it is best to offer the engaged couple several options. Brief descriptions of some typical program choices follow. These descriptions are provided to assist you in describing the programs as clearly and completely as possible.

Diocesan Marriage Preparation Programs

Many large, urban dioceses have developed ongoing marriage preparation programs (ie, Pre-Cana), which provide reliable, up-to-date premarriage education for engaged couples. The programs usually consist of an evening or weekend conference with several sessions conducted by trained priests and married couples. The groups are usually large and the format includes leader presentations, group discussions, and communications exercises. Topics discussed include sacramentality, adjustment in marriage, love, communication, sexuality, money, and children.

The diocesan program is probably the best and simplest means through which the couple fulfills the requirement to participate in a structured premarriage preparation program. If such a program is available in your diocese or in a nearby diocese, you can give the couple a schedule of upcoming programs during the first session so that the couple can schedule attendance as soon as possible.

Encounter Weekends

Perhaps the least well-known (and least available) of the premarriage education programs are Encounters for the Engaged, Engaged Encounters, Discovery Weekends, or Tobit Weekends, etc. If such a program is available in your diocese, or within reasonable distance, it might be an excellent opportunity for couples to deepen their communication and love in a setting that encourages mutual trust and openness.

This type of program is effective because the couple makes the effort to get away from stress and distraction and commit time to be with one another; the couple receives tremendous warmth, caring, and support from the experienced priests and couples conducting the program; emphasis is placed on their married life, not on the wedding; and the couple focuses on aspects of their relationship that they might never consider on their own. The format of the program includes insightful presentations; time for private reflections, preferably written; conversations in which partners share ideas and feelings; and structured progression from "I" to "We" and to God and others.

Topics frequently covered include the following:

- building confidence and skill in communication;
- adjustment and the stages of relationship;
- areas for deeper understanding, eg, money, time, mutual goals;
- sex and sexuality;
- vocation and sacrament; and
- openness to the world.

These weekends often involve several paraliturgies which are especially designed for the weekend, and they often close with Mass on Sunday.

Parish-Based Premarriage Programs

Although parish-based programs are relatively rare, they might be more common in a diocese with rural or relatively isolated parishes than in a large metropolitan diocese where other programs are readily available. However, the availability of other programs in urban areas does not mean that parish-based programs are not appropriate and useful. They can be an excellent alternative to diocesan-sponsored programs.

Usually conducted by married couples in the parish and one or more parish priests, parish-based programs are held in parish facilities or married couples' homes. Unlike diocesan programs and encounter weekends, the parish-based program is designed for small groups and relies chiefly on informal discussion. The chief benefits of the parish-based program are listed on the following page.

- Designed for very small groups and thus quite flexible in assessing and meeting the needs of individual couples.

- The parish priest can stay in close touch and know precisely how well the program is doing and be apprised quickly of problems and special needs that a particular couple might have.

- Couples are befriended by the people running the program and thus experience great personal caring and support from the local church community.

- The program can easily be tailored to the level of couples served by the parish.

- Valuable spinoffs include individual counseling for the bride-to-be by one of the women in the program or advice on money matters or career opportunities for the groom-to-be by one of the men. Such contacts often continue long after the couple is married.

- It is possible to follow couples and consider post-marital programs (eg, six and 12 months after the wedding).

- The program can easily have a social component (ie, the priest invites all the couples planning marriage within a given period of time to a monthly beer and pizza party to introduce them to the parish team.) This approach helps the young couples become friends and perhaps diminishes feelings of isolation that some newly-married couples might experience.

The challenges of the parish-based program include identifying, screening, selecting, and training couples on the parish team so that the program is successful. Local couples might not have the image of experts or an aura of competence and credibility. Some engaged couples say that this does not bother them; rather, they feel they can share their experience with "plain folk" and they are not intimidated. Others are turned off by "old Bernie and Betsy" and ask, What are we doing here? We aren't going to learn much from these two.

Many maintain, however, and we agree, that the couples must be as highly qualified as possible. Not only should they be warm, sympathetic, intelligent, flexible, and reasonably articulate, they must be well-read in marriage and family; able to put forth interesting, relevant, practical presentations; and experts in leading discussions.

Parish couples in the premarriage program should know the tools (games, tests, involvement instruments) available to them and when, how, and whether to use them. If the couples have career experience that gives them credibility and competence, so much the better, provided they realize their role is primarily one of encouraging couples to reflect and communicate with each other.

APPENDIX B

B

Questions

The questions presented in this Appendix are a helpful resource for the priest during interviews with engaged couples. Only a few of these questions should be used as prompters. In fact, you most likely will use this only to help you frame your own, even better, questions.

Questions should be discretely woven into conversation, not spilled out in rapid-fire interrogation like F. Lee Bailey during cross-examination.

For those of you who would like to consider designing a brief inventory that each partner might fill out separately as a basis for later discussion, some of these questions might serve as a starting point.

Relationship

How did you meet? When? Where? (Tell me about it!)

What two qualities first attracted you to him/her?

Had you done much serious dating prior to meeting each other?

Have you ever been engaged before? (What broke it up? How long ago?)

When did you begin to "go steady?"

When did you begin to think seriously about marriage? Who brought it up?

Did the decision require pondering, or did it come easily?

How long have you been engaged?

Have you had many quarrels or serious disagreements? What were they about usually?

How did you go about patching them up? (Who starts the reconciliation process? Who gives in?)

Have you broken off your engagement at any time? (What brought that about? What brought you back together?)

What have you learned about yourself, your partner, the need for adjustment since you've known each other?

What attitude (fault or habit) do you wish your partner would change? What attitude would your partner wish you to change?

What trait (quality or skill) do you wish your partner would develop further?

Friends and Family

Tell me about your families.

94

How many brothers and sisters?

Where do you fit in?

How do you get along?

What are your parents like?

How do they get along with each other?

Are your parents divorced or separated? (When? How did it affect you?)

What does your father/mother do?

What was it like growing up? Any unusual problems or special situations?

How do they feel about your fiance?

How did they react to your intention to marry? (Objection? Support?)

What about your future inlaws? See any potential trouble spots?

Are you the kind of person who makes close friends?

How do your friends feel about your marriage? (Your fiance?)

Health

Have you ever been under a doctor's care?
(What for?)

Have you ever been hospitalized? (What for? How recently? What is the present prognosis?)

Are you taking medication on a regular basis? (What kind? What for?)

Is there a great deal of stress in your life? (What are its sources? How do you handle it?)

What about your (his/her) use of alcohol? (Drugs?) Is it considerable? (Is it something that worries you?) Have you (he/she) tried to cut down? Is it something you have discussed? Would like to discuss?

Have you ever had psychological (psychiatric) counseling or therapy? (Occasional? Intermittent? Regular?) What are your feelings about its success? Are you presently involved in such counseling? Were you ever hospitalized for psychological problems?

How would you describe your state of health?

Sexuality

How would you describe your attitude toward sex?

How would you describe the state of your sexual knowledge and education?

Did your parents discuss sex? (Negatively? Positively?)

Could you say a few words on the importance of sex in marriage?

What kinds of problems regarding sex do you think couples have in the early years of marriage?

How do you think couples can best handle problems in sexual adjustment?

Over the years of marriage who is more interested in sex, husbands or wives?

Compatibility

Do your philosophies of life fit together fairly well? (How do you know?)

What are your short-term and long-term goals for yourself, your relationship, your career?

What kind of person would you like to be? Please don't answer in terms of achievement—but, rather, in terms of qualities.

Do you share numerous common interests that are important to both of you? Are those which you do not share more numerous? What are your dislikes?

Do you perceive and interpret things similarly—problems, people, social issues, political questions?

Do you like most of his/her friends? (His/her job?)

What is your preferred way of spending an evening, weekend, vacation?

Sex Roles

How is the role of women (men) changing? Is change good or bad?

Do you expect your husband to do chores? To what extent? Do you, as husband, agree?

How long should a wife keep a full-time job (pursue a demanding career)? Can you foresee any stresses here?

What is left of the concept of husband as head of the house?

How will you resolve questions when you hold contradictory viewpoints?

Is there a leader in a marriage? Who gets the job? When?

How is money handled, spent, accounted for?

Which of you is more dominant? Which of you is more competent? In what areas?

Religion

Are religious values important in your life? How do they influence you?

Have you read anything—other than newspaper pieces—about religion (not ESP, EST, or the occult) recently?

What can religion do for people?

Why is it important for people to worship together?

Have the two of you ever talked about your faith or your faith differences?

To what extent do you practice your faith?

What is your perception of God? Do you pray? How? When?

Are Church rules and God's Will different?

How would you describe your conscience?

What does a religious ceremony do for a marriage?

Communication

Is it easy to talk to each other? Do you run out of topics? Can you listen? (Even to trivia?)

Are there certain things you would rather not bring up? Why? Are there areas your partner is especially sensitive about?

Does he/she try to "shape you up" (nag, demand)?

Are you assertive enough (aggressive, honest)?

Have you given (received) the silent treatment?

Have you been irritated or angry with each other? Do you believe anger, etc, is the result of threat?

Can you forgive and apologize? (Too easily?) Do you stockpile your partner's faults and mistakes?

Have you used the excuse "That's just the way I am?"

Do you have the courage (sense) to tell your partner what you want or what's bothering you? Or do you just expect him/her to know?

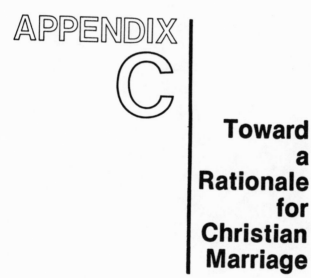

APPENDIX
C

**Toward
a
Rationale
for
Christian
Marriage**

Catholic belief in irrevocable marriage vows is integral to the Christian law of love.

God loves us, both saint and sinner, with a constant, limitless love—one which led Jesus to the cross for people who, with few exceptions, either hated Him or did not even know Him. In return, God invites love from us, a *total* love for Him and for our fellow man and woman. On our own, we are incapable of such love; however, through His love—given directly by Him and given through our fellows—we too can develop a more than human capacity for love.

That God's fidelity in love towards mankind and the human commitment of love in marriage are used to explain each other is no accident. In Matthew 19, Jesus describes these commitments in similar ways. Jesus explained the need for a total commitment in response to the rich young man's question, "What good must I do to possess everlasting life?" Jesus pointed to the Commandments. The young man asked, "What else?" Jesus replied that if he wished to complete the task, he must sell all he owned, give the proceeds to the poor, and follow him into the unknown.

The young man went away and Jesus commented on how difficult it is for the rich to enter the Kingdom. In contrast, he promised many rewards and eternal life to those who give up kin, possessions, and land for Him. In a word, whoever would follow Jesus must quit home—that is, security, safety, support, esteem—and go wandering with Him among the world's strangers, prowling after those in need.

Law and Love

Jesus repeatedly repudiates legalistic religion, under which the adherent could carefully calculate what was "owed" to God. The Jew felt that the Law was a relief, not a burden, for it set limits on what was expected of him. To come before the living God one day was dreadful enough; but it was far worse and more terrifying to do so without a clear idea of the terms on which one would be judged. The more explicit the Law, the better the boon.

In contrast, Jesus tells His followers that they will be judged according to their *service* to others—feeding the hungry, clothing the naked, and caring for the sick. He disdains legalistic limits, or any limits at all. At no point can one say that he has satisfied God's claim. God's claims are measured, not by a specific set of commandments or duties, but by the limitless misery and need of all human beings and by the limitless love Jesus proclaimed. The disciples, staggered by the great demands of love, asked, "Who then, can be saved?" Jesus answered, "With man, it is impossible, but for God, all things are possible."

Truly Open Marriage

A similar, open-ended commitment is required in marriage, as we learn in the same chapter of Matthew. Jesus states that, even if a man is cuckolded, abandoned, and suffers the worst imaginable misfortune—being left childless, no better than a eunuch—even then he should stand fast and be faithful. This is crazy, his disciples warn, and impossible besides! Few would risk a marriage that allowed no escape. New, yes; insane, no, rejoins Jesus. It is one of those outrageous, glorious things that God can help the human heart be capable of.

A marriage that can be dissolved is a marriage of qualified, conditional, "if" love, just as a religion that simple requires adherence to a detailed set of laws is a religion of conditional love. Open-ended commitment transforms both religion and marriage; whereas each had formerly been determined by law, in the Christian vision, each would be determined by human need and "divine" generosity.

The Chicken or The Egg

Irrevocable vows are also sharply different from more sentimentalized, romantic views of marriage. With total commitment a man and woman pledge themselves, not to joy, peace, or satisfaction, but to *fidelity*—from which joy, peace, and satisfaction are believed to spring. They do not seek their delight and hope it will carry them through duty. They opt for duty and accept the delight that it will bring. In this way, they imitate God's love, and work toward their mutual growth and sanctification.

Pledging

It is an ancient observation that we humans arrive in life caring only about ourselves and that we uncannily are disposed to stay that way. It is an ancient Christian belief that with God's help—and the help of others, too—we can and must grow out of selfcenteredness into love. One of the most potent strategies for emerging from egotism into love is pledging. To pledge is to put oneself at another's service, *to give someone a claim upon yourself.*

Pledge yourself truly to another and you are doubly constrained. You are now obliged to be of service, no matter how you or your circumstances or your pledge-person change and grow, the measure of your giving becomes not your own preference, but the other's need. Let another claim you, and the immensity and urgency of that claim lie beyond your control. In short, a pledged person is repeatedly summoned to greater cherishing than he or she planned, envisioned, or even intended; they are called to "play over their heads"—to love beyond themselves.

Pledging and Freedom

Pledging appears to be a yielding of one's freedom. It is really a path that renders life more voluntary. Precisely by rising to meet one's commitments, a person grows to have a greater and more giving will.

There is always fear that once pledges are made, the other person will change. Affection, trust, and delight may then dissolve, leaving one bound to carry out commitments joylessly or alone. Those held back by this fear imagine that it is attraction to another which supports fidelity and makes it agreeable. The contrary is more often true. It is in keeping

106

our pledges to people that we invite them to be even more attractive than we had first seen or they had first been. Affection is a weak and fickle foundation for service; service, though, is the best possible ground for the continued growth of affection. In keeping pledges, then, we increase our capacity to love and help others increase their capacity to love.

No Illusions

Christian marriage is the most awesome pledge that one human being can give another: for better, for worse, until death. Its only model is the faith we pledge to the Lord or better still, the faith that God, fidelity Himself, pledges to us. The relationship between man and woman is as the relationship between disciple and Jesus: one is loved, will be loved, can claim love, whatever one's faults. When true conjugal love blossoms, neither wife nor husband need be anxious about whether they will continue to be cherished. He or she is totally accepted and literally forgiven before any fall.

The Church offers no illusions that such a commitment is easy. All Christian sacramental pledges are taken in the shadow of the cross and none lead us away from suffering. No pledge is great unless it passes through fire and sorrow. Pledged marriage is a little like childbirth: Afterwards, everyone says how marvelous it was, but it took pain and struggle to get there.

Pledging and Growth

Christian tradition is skeptical about a person's ability to come to fully maturity or to possess life without pledging himself to other people; for better, for worse, until death. We are stubbornly selfish creatures who are not likely to grow unless challenged, confronted, and committed. To pledge without recourse is to expose ourselves to risk—but to a risk that was there already. For what it takes to serve our pledge-person when they are ill-tempered, ungrateful, mean, and infuritating is nothing more than the qualities we must acquire if we are to grow up.

It is difficult to serve anyone, more difficult when the terms of service are unspecified, and most difficult when there is no end to the service. Only one thing in the world is more difficult: to serve only those one likes, to the extent that it is agreeable, and for just as long as one pleases. This is not difficult; it is impossible. *For on these unpledged terms we end up serving no one but ourselves.*

An important decision in marrying is selecting the right partner. An even more crucial one is choosing *how* to marry the person of your choice. It is not usual to discover major marital "incompatibilities" beyond anyone's control; they tend to be very basic human faults that no one *wishes* to control. Pledge marriage encourages and demands that the partners who understand and pledge irrevocable love and service will find themselves growing in age and grace and wisdom—and commitment is the rich soil in which this growth is rooted.

The basic question for those who counsel couples contemplating marriage, then, is whether the couple has the insight to say "together forever" and the courage to mean it.

APPENDIX
D

**Some
Special
Issues**

Living Together Before Marriage

The incidence of living together varies and probably occurs less frequently in older, more traditional parishes and more frequently in parishes where the number of single, college, and professional people is higher.

The first problem about the situation is that you probably will not find out about it. If you do, it will be because the couple gives the same address or because they tell you about it, in which case you might try to understand their motives for doing so. Are they defiant and challenging the values for which you stand; are they getting it off their chests; or are they simply being matter-of-fact about it?

Whatever the case, tongue-clucking and severe disapproval are useless. A better approach is to walk the narrow line between condoning and overt condemnation (which would very likely turn them off), while trying to explore what the experience means to them. A response like, "Well, I understand arrangements like that are not so uncommon anymore," followed by some pertinent questions, could prove fruitful.

How did it come about?

How has it been working out?

What are the factors that led you to decide to marry at this time?

Tell me, how do you think marriage will differ from your present situation? What kind of change in attitude or commitment will it involve?

Why is it important for you to formalize your relationship?

Do you BOTH want to marry or is one of you nudging the other?

What effects (negative or positive) do you think your experience will have on your marriage?

You know I represent a special, rich, and rather demanding religious tradition of marriage and, as you most likely also know, that tradition frowns on people living together before marriage. Perhaps you can understand how your situation makes me a little uncomfortable about whether you are serious about a religious marriage with its implications of fidelity and permanence. Can you add anything to help my discomfort?

These questions should elicit helpful information to make an informed judgment about the couple. No one can blueprint just how to move with this situation, but here are a few more points to consider. Don't let the fact that the couple has set up housekeeping take center stage and obscure the good attributes and qualities they probably have going for them. If they are relatively young and living together was entered into precipitously on short acquaintance, it will be much more disconcerting than if they are older and began to live together after mature and serious consideration.

Couples brought up in certain environments might, in some instances, begin living together without ever applying moral qualifiers to the situation. If they believe there is NO significant difference between living together, with its loopholes and escape hatches, and the "together forever" commitment of marriage, this is a troubling factor. The fact that they now WANT to marry may well stand as evidence that they and their relationship have matured.

Some priests say a religious marriage ceremony should not take place unless the couple agrees to separate until they are married—strange sounding condition. Others say that a discussion of the bonding effect of sexual relations and the special intimacy and excitement of the first days of marriage might be pursued—together with the suggestion that some kind of real and symbolic fresh start for this new and different relationship should certainly be considered. Some priests might subtract points for the unconventional lifestyle; others might add points for the couple's honesty in bringing up the matter at all.

Inflation

A factor that cannot be ignored in marriage preparation is inflation. In a very real sense, it is a Christian problem. When it reaches the levels it has reached in the last several years, and threatens still to rise further, inflation devastates our attempts to control the future, to predict or expect.

Inflation rewards short-term consumption and reinforces the tenets of the "Now" generation. People who have saved prudently for five years to put a substantial downpayment on a house now can barely afford the blueprints. On the other hand, those who spent imprudently on a car or an outsized diamond ring have seen the value of their purchases soar. Inflation has made a mockery of our traditional notions of planning and preparation.

Inflation has also made many people anxious and fearful, and it has stimulated the impetus to acquire things and protect what one has already. It is simply assumed that the young wife will work fulltime and earn as much as she possibly can. The obvious stress that this puts on marriage is ignored, although it is safe to assume that women have become habituated to the role of working outside the home in the past twenty-five years. Many have the talent and ability to cope with working, and many derive significant satisfaction from having a career.

Some Pollyannas who say money is not important might be dismayed to learn that a direct correlation exists between adequate income and marital happiness and stability.

Interfaith Marriage

The Church's approach to interfaith couples has experienced quite an evolution over the past twenty-five years. For example, it was not usual for the non-Catholic partner to be required to attend six instructional sessions with the priest before the couple could marry. Such rigid and formal orientation programs are uncommon today.

Nevertheless, the faith difference is still an important topic to work through with an interfaith couple. The subject should be met head-on at the first session with the engaged interfaith couple.

The first session probably is the non-Catholic's first contact with a priest or first visit to a rectory. This might cause general uneasiness. In addition, unspoken tension might exist between the couple and the priest regarding the interfaith situation. The couple might be waiting on pins and needles for you to ask the question, Are you both Catholic? They might be unable to relax and concentrate on other matters until the subject is brought out in the open.

As soon as you are aware that you are working with an interfaith couple, take steps to help the couple relax and discuss their situation openly. You might let them know that you are familiar with the non-Catholic's religion, or with his or her Church or pastor. Inform the couple of requirements and expectations regarding their interfaith marriage. Do this gently with openers similar to: You probably have been wondering how the Church regards interfaith marriage... let's review these viewpoints together.

Acknowledge the fact that problems exist and encourage the couple to verbalize their fears. For example, many couples need help working out the differences that will affect the practice of their different religions—What will we do on Sundays? How do we establish a common religious life? How can I support my partner in his or her Faith? Help the interfaith couple share their religious traditions. Acknowledge that these traditions might be a potential source of tension, but encourage the couple to view them as a source of enrichment in their marriage. For example, you might discuss a typical wedding ceremony in both churches. Or, for some couples, an open discussion of faith and doctrinal differences might be appropriate. Many couples will discover that they bring religious prejudice to their marriages, ie, preconceived notions about their partner's faith. Point out that only by airing their notions and sharing their knowledge will they become comfortable with each other's form of worship.

Beware of religious indifference, whether deliberate or unconscious. Some couples might deliberately play down their faith differences in order to minimize potential problems in their relationship. Gently illustrate how this might not always be possible when, for example, children, parents, and death enter the picture. Other couples, through no fault of their own, have unconsciously made their faith difference a forbidden territory. Encourage them not to gloss over differences but to take a good, hard look at them so they can deepen and strengthen their relationship against tension and pressure. Three typical points of tension and pressure are discussed below.

Family. When parents and other family members exert pressure, thoughtfulness, and diplomacy are essential. Remind the couple that their purpose should be to gain acceptance of their marriage, not win arguments. You might offer to meet with the families or with the non-Catholic minister to ease their way. Discourage the attitude that, 'We couldn't care less.' Help them find a way to work things out with as little bitterness and regret as possible.

The Wedding. Often, the Catholic partner has strong feelings about what he or she wants in the ceremony—whether it is a Nuptial Mass or part of a Mass. The Eucharist may not always be appropriate in interfaith marriages, and the priest can help the couple choose a liturgy which expresses unity and with which all can be comfortable. In some cases, the Catholic Church might be totally unacceptable for members of the non-Catholic partner's family as a setting for the ceremony (ie, I wouldn't set foot in a Catholic Church). In such cases, another religious setting or a secular setting can be chosen and approved. Under all circumstances, the non-Catholic should be encouraged to participate and make decisions about the wedding. He or she should be informed that a minister of his faith can participate in the ceremony.

Children. Couples should be urged to face the question of the relHgous education of their children. A little role playing might help them foresee any problems. You might say, Imagine that your first child, a boy, is five years old. The Catholic school is close to your home, and tuition is not a problem. Will you send him to the Catholic school? Your children want mommy and daddy to go to Mass. They do not understand why you cannot attend Church together. How do you handle this?

Second Marriages

At your first meeting with the engaged couple, determine whether either partner has been married before. This information often will surface in the course of your initial conversation with the couple, either as a forthright statement of fact or through jokes and innuendos.

Keep your ears open and assume nothing. Sometimes people who have been married outside of the Church fail to mention the marriage because they think that it "does not count" in the eyes of the Church. Of course, it counts very much, especially in terms of marriage preparation. Moreover, it can be embarrassing and painful to the couple and to you if knowledge of a previous marriage does not surface until so late in marriage preparation that plans are tangled or the marriage preparation schedule is delayed.

Some priests shy away from discussing the previous marriage simply to prevent the couple from feeling uncomfortable. With tact and compassion you can encourage the couple to talk about the previous marriage, even if the experience was painful. How comfortably and thoroughly the couple can discuss painful or delicate aspects of the previous marriage in your presence is a good indicator both of the distance from the former marriage and the strength of the relationship that the engaged couple has established. During your conversation, watch and listen to the other partner closely. How does he or she feel about the previous marriage? Do special concerns and apprehensions exist? (They usually do.)

If the previously married partner has been divorced only recently, consider this a red flag. The couple might be moving too quickly, and the previously married partner might be "jumping from the frying pan into the fire," so to speak. It takes time to heal the pain and sorrow that occurs after a marriage fails. For some, the healing process takes years, and painful scars remain despite the time involved. Remarriage need not be discouraged, but a certain amount of caution is advisable to avoid repetition of pain.

Statistics on divorce are high enough to warrant helping people take a long, hard look at each other and at the institution of marriage. Remarriage should not, and cannot, be a solution to bad marriages. Without being a "killjoy," we can help people recognize that remarriage should be considered carefully.

The Matter of Children

Children from a previous marriage (or marriages) often create a special problem for the engaged couple. Parents want to please both their children and themselves. When the children oppose the marriage, however, parents cannot do both. Discuss everyone's feelings, including the children's. How does the other partner feel about the fiance's children and their attitude toward the marriage? What arrangements and agreements have been made? In these situations, it often is difficult to encourage both partners to express what is on their minds, what they dislike, etc. You might consider talking with each partner separately and encouraging each of them to talk more openly with the other.

Annulments

Frequently, couples have only just begun the annulment process when they come to arrange the wedding date. Be careful. Most marriage tribunals are adamant about not setting a wedding date until after the annulment has been granted. This fact can be explained to the couple carefully by pointing out the obvious problems and anxieties that can occur when arrangements have been made but the annulment has not been approved. Although couples can become quite impatient and irritated, setting or promising dates without paper in hand could precipitate even more anger and hurt in the long run.

As a matter of course, ask to see the official papers when an annulment already has been granted. The document might contain important information (such as the stipulation that requires counseling before a person can remarry in

the Church). Make certain from the outset that everything
is clear.

In the Case of Death

If the previously married partner's spouse died, encourage him or her to talk about the experience so you can
evaluate the level of grief. The widowed partner also must
experience the healing process before entering another marriage. Grief over the death of a spouse often prompts the
widowed partner to marry quickly without due consideration of the strength of the new relationship. The eagerness
to remarry often is prompted by the need for someone to care
for them and/or support their children.

Tread carefully. Don't darken any happiness that the
couple has found in each other unless you are quite certain
from what has been said that one or the other is not ready to
marry.

Children

The subject of children is an important dimension of
marriage preparation because the Church considers procrea-
tion a significant reason for the existence of the sacrament
of marriage. To ignore the topic would do a great disservice
to the couple because children encompass some of the greatest joys and difficulties of married life. Moreover, looking
ahead, the Church has a responsibility to children—even
those yet unborn—to encourage their welfare, their existence, and their spiritual well-being and education.

Although engaged couples frequently appear reluctant to discuss children, this does not mean that they are against having them. If they seem vague and disinterested, it may be that the prospect of having children seems rather remote; they might not have given children much thought. Point out the value of being prepared to cope with decisions and changes so they are not merely carried along with the tide. Mention that the desire to recreate their love is basic, very strong, and frequently outweighs any rational decision to wait to have children. Although they might now believe that they will not have children for five-to-seven years, the odds are that they will have at least one child during that period of time.

Natural Family Planning

Find out when they are "planning" to have children and proceed from there. Again, you might point out that the decision to have children ultimately is not only reasoned and rational, but emotional, based on their desire for and love of one another.

The couple might be reluctant to discuss children because they intend to practice artificial birth control; they might feel uncomfortable about this decision because of the Church's teachings. If you sense that this is the case, or if they tell you as much, take the opportunity to discuss and explain the Church's views on birth control and the value of children. This might also be the moment to explain Natural Family Planning (NFP). Many couples, although reluctant to turn to contraception, do so because they are unaware of any other method available to them.

121

At any rate, acknowledge that our society is oriented toward contraception, and most couples have grown to adulthood familiar with this orientation. Point out that the freedom to postpone childbearing with any certainty is a relatively new concept and carries with it a burden—how to decide. You might ask them about their decision-making process, and you might point out the dangers of loving in a contraceptive society, ie, self-centeredness, emptiness, greed, etc. (A good way to develop the topic of moral decision-making in marriage is to discuss the basis on which people should decide to have children.) Beyond the decision of *having* children, and when, is the matter of childrearing. Because couples tend to think only of the first few years of their marital life, encourage them to share their ideas and fears about raising children.

Joy of Children

Discuss the experiences that helped form these ideas and fears. Ask each of them, What characteristics, qualities, or behavior patterns in your mothers and fathers would you prefer not to imitate? Which *would* you imitate or emulate? Although seemingly obvious, mention some of the implications of having children. Because "implications" always sound negative, discuss the gratifications as well.

Throughout the marriage preparation program, your objective is to help the couple examine their feelings and look to their future with realism and foresight. Try to make them see that marriage is replete with unknowns, not the least of which is children. (When they should have them; if they should have them; how many; what they will be like, etc.) End the discussion on a positive note, pointing out that children should be viewed as gifts, guests, treasures, and privileges—not subjects for prediction, manipulation, or indifference.

Convalidations

Requests for convalidations come from couples who were married by a judge in a civil ceremony, are free to marry in the Church, and would like to have their marriage blessed or recognized by the Church.

Most common policies or marriage guidelines state that couples who request convalidations should be treated as any other couple who wishes to marry in the Church. However, pastoral response should be dictated by "who they are."

Consider the following questions to determine the type of convalidation case before you.

Was the civil marriage held recently?

Was the couple married in a civil ceremony because another priest wanted them to delay their marriage?

Are they seeking to have their marriage blessed in the belief that they have you over a barrel, ie, Do you want us to continue living in sin, etc?

Does the couple appear to have a strong marital relationship?

Does the couple have a basic understanding of the religious dimension of marriage?

In all cases, but especially in the case of a well-established marriage of several years duration, ask, What has brought you to this decision?

Is the decision to request convalidation mutual?

Do one or both partners need a reconciliation with the Church?

Preparation Programs

When the couple has been married recently, insist that they undertake the normal marriage preparation program. Spend time with them to determine the strength of the relationship, and help them increase that strength.

For couples who have been married for several years and appear to have a good relationship, total marriage preparation is out of place. However, spend some time discussing the religious dimension of marriage. To illustrate the meaning of Christian marriage, call upon their own marriage experience, asking questions similar to the following:

How does the example of Christ influence your marriage?

How does the example of Christ influence your relationship with your children?

How do you function as Christians in your community?

To what extent do you participate in parish community worship?

No matter what the circumstances, do not allow convalidation to be rushed; do not go through the motions of a "quickie" blessing. Take time to allow the couple to learn about and appreciate the sacramental aspects of the new marriage vows that they will be taking.

Pregnancy

Ministering to the average engaged couple is always challenging, but ministering to the couple who faces pregnancy before marriage tests all of your skills and resources. Considered a motivation to marry for centuries, pregnancy today signals the need for extensive counseling and, in many cases, indicates reasons to delay or refuse marriage.

Age and Maturity

If the couple is mature and accepting of the situation; if they have a sound relationship and had fully intended to marry in the near future; if they have insight into the stress that a child can place on the early months of marriage; if their financial situation is reasonably sound; if they can count on emotional and practical support from family and friends, then marriage *might* be appropriate.

On the other hand, if the couple is young and immature, feels trapped, and is visibly shaken by the pregnancy; if the girl wants the baby, but the boy is clearly uneasy; if they both feel that the situation is unfair; if marriage has not been considered or was only a remote possibility before pregnancy; if their financial situation is tenuous; if pregnancy interrupts or destroys other plans (ie, school, higher education, a career); marriage is ill-advised.

The priest's primary role will be to identify positive alternatives, spell them out in detail, and support them by contacting and arranging for the expectant mother's care, the birth of the baby, the adoption of the baby, etc. You might offer to meet with the families, and you might suggest ways in which the expectant father can remain in the picture so that the young, unwed couple can reassess their relationship later, if they wish.

Emotional Responses

Pregnancy can place the priest under pressure from the couple, their parents, and even their relatives. Guilt, resentment, anger, shame, and fear will fill the rectory parlor. Often, when we try to help the couple and their respective families handle the crisis, anger and threats surface—and recriminations. Nothing is to be done but to try and understand the pain that everyone is experiencing. Don't succumb to the pressure and marry the couple against your better judgment; neither should you give up and suggest that they "get married in city hall."

If you have reasoned that the decision to marry is a poor one, share your concern with the couple—and with the parents, if appropriate. If you refuse to marry the couple, do not allow them or their families to place responsibility for alternative action on your shoulders (ie, living together, marrying outside the Church, abortion, etc). Keep in mind that they are free to make their own decisions; and remind the couple that they are responsible for how they use that freedom.

A Note on Professional Counseling

A couple needs counseling and time to sort things out. Sometimes, however, a couple cannot even tolerate the thought of six-to-eight weeks in a counseling program. One or two sessions that are attended merely to appease the priest will not help the couple and will only make the counselor's task difficult. If counseling sessions are available through the diocese, they are valuable resources that should be considered but that should not be forced upon the couple.

An Afterword

As you have seen, this book contains specific, practical details designed to help parish ministers in their work with engaged couples. It is our belief that these details are important, and that attention to them can influence the effectiveness of premarriage ministry.

It is important for us to remember, however, that while information can be provided, and strategies mastered, the all-important insight, caring, and support must come from us. We will continually need to remind ourselves that these two people are unique...their marriage will be unique. It never is "just another wedding."

The effective premarriage minister will, periodically, need to bolster his conviction that time spent caring for engaged couples is necessary. Any effort to help strengthen marriage is always worthwhile. The point can't be overemphasized: engagement is an opportunity—both for the couple and for the church—to care for people.

Engagement is only the first season of marriage. As the popular song "We've Only Just Begun" implies, there is *much more to come*. Couples need the care and interest of the church through all the seasons of their marriage. We need to find ways at this time not only to build relationships, but to continue them...to strengthen 'belonging' and help couples find ways and resources to keep their love dynamic, alive, and growing.

Other Effective Tools for Premarriage Ministry

BEGINNING YOUR MARRIAGE - Standard Edition

BEGINNING YOUR MARRIAGE - Interfaith Edition
Paperback books dealing with sacramentality, fidelity, intimacy, personal growth, communication and sex.
By Rev. John L. Thomas, S.J. (1980 Ed.)

EL CAMINO HACIA EL AMOR
Spanish adaptation of "Beginning Your Marriage".

PERSPECTIVES ON MARRIAGE

Workbook for the engaged. Exercises in communication skills, money management and liturgy planning. An update of the Pre-Cana Packet.

ADVENTURE TOGETHER

Six-cassette premarriage education program geared to 16-20 year olds. Complete with teacher's manuals.

HERE WE ARE

A two-cassette introduction to the Catholic faith for persons entering an interfaith marriage.

Available from: Buckley Publications, Inc.
233 E. Erie Street
Chicago, IL 60611
(312) 943-2066